Mary

Published by
The Bible Reading Fellowship
15 The Chambers, Vineyard
Abingdon, OX14 3FE
United kingdom
Tel: +44 (0)1865 319700
Email: enquiries@brf.org.uk
Website: www.brf.org.uk
BRF is a Registered Charity

ISBN 978 1 84101 651 1
First published 2014
10 9 8 7 6 5 4 3 2 1 0

Acknowledgments
Unless otherwise stated, scripture quotations are taken from The New Revised Standard Version of the Bible, Anglicised Edition, copyright © 1989, 1995 by the Division of Christian Education of the National Council of the Churches of Christ in the USA, are used by permission. All rights reserved.

Extracts from the Authorised Version of the Bible (The King James Bible), the rights in which are vested in the Crown, are reproduced by permission of the Crown's patentee, Cambridge University Press.

Cover image: Wong Yu Liang/Shutterstock

Every effort has been made to trace and contact copyright owners for material used in this resource. We apologise for any inadvertent omissions or errors, and would ask those concerned to contact us so that full acknowledgment can be made in the future.

A catalogue record for this book is available from the British Library

Printed and bound by CPI Group (UK) Ltd, Croydon CR0 4YY

Mary

A gospel witness to transfiguration and liberation

Andrew Jones

To my nieces, Gwenllian, Lowri and Yasmin, just embarking on the adventure of life—go joyfully and faithfully.

Acknowledgements

A number of people have journeyed with me while I have been writing this book. I would like to thank those with whom I worship week by week in the Bro Enlli Ministry Area and the Archdeaconry of Meirionnydd. They have listened patiently to me as I have tested and explored many of my ideas about Mary, and several of them have challenged some of my opinions. Such patience and challenge have been a significant impetus. Also I thank my colleagues in the Diocese of Bangor and especially the Bishop's Council with whom I share ministry—Bishop Andy John, Sion Rhys Evans, Sue Jones, Paul Davies and Mike West. They have teased me endlessly about my preoccupation with Mary but such teasing kept me digging more and more into her story. I have also valued my conversations about the possibilities of the human Mary with Fraser Paterson and with two of my aunts, Lowri Hulse and Gwennie Johnson. I am again grateful to Naomi Starkey and BRF for the original invitation to embark on what has been a fascinating journey of discovery.

Contents

Foreword 6
Introduction 7

Part 1: Threshold of transfiguration 13
Chapter 1: Songs and cries of Hebrew children 21
Chapter 2: New Testament variations on Mary 39

Part 2: Liberating signs of the kingdom of God 55
Chapter 3: Divinely chosen, kingdom worker 65
Chapter 4: Virgin mother, profoundly human 83

Part 3: Bearer of the incarnation, witness to the resurrection 99
Chapter 5: Light shining from Nazareth 109
Chapter 6: Anguish at the foot of the cross 125

Part 4: Abiding voice of freedom 141
Chapter 7: Witnessing God's transfiguring power 151
Chapter 8: Challenges from Christ's final prayer in John 170

Afterword 187
Questions for group discussion and reflection 191
References 197

Foreword

Mary, the mother of Jesus, has been the object of human projection and idealisation and, throughout Christian history, people have made of her what suited them. For many women, Mary has been a symbol of oppression, of female passivity and subjugation, an impossible ideal of perfect motherhood and a denial of female sexuality. For others, she has been variously the Mary of the psyche, bearer of great burdens, Mary the feminine principle in humankind, Mary the object of devotion.

But when we go back to the Bible, is there a Mary we can meet with confidence? Andrew Jones invites us to encounter Mary, a flesh-and-blood woman who lived through extraordinary events, in the context of liberation, and to read hers as a story of transfiguration. She is representative of the *anawim*, the little people, the poor and marginalised who suffer and wait for liberation, and her 'yes' to God in the incarnation is a story of *theosis*, of a world radically changed by God's transfiguring grace, and of the possibility of human beings entering into the divine nature through that grace.

Mary's is the great New Testament song of liberation. In the Magnificat, she anticipates the nature of the glory and celebrates it. Mary is the prophet of the poor, announcing the transformed social order. The spiritual realm is embedded in economic and political reality, and so it still is today.

Kathy Galloway
Head of Christian Aid Scotland
Leader of the Iona Community 2002–09

Introduction

In some ways for me the idea of writing a book on Mary has actually grown out of some negative feelings. For a long time I have been generally unhappy that a key Gospel player occupies a kind of second division role in the life of some Christian traditions. Too often I have heard comments such as 'Oh, she doesn't belong to us' or 'We don't worship Mary like they do; we worship Christ' or 'She served her purpose in bringing Christ into the world; she has no continuing ministry'. I can see the direction from which this kind of talk emerges and the historical influences that have come to bear on these ideas, but I have always been uncomfortable with them, even to the extent that I think they are essentially misguided. For many years I have felt uneasy about listening to comments that make Mary, the mother of Christ, a contentious figure.

In much the same way I have been uncomfortable with an oversimplistic approach to reading about Mary in the Gospels. It is as if some people feel the need to scratch around in order to salvage any kind of honourable feature of her character. By doing so, there is the risk of simply being content to say that Mary was humble, obedient and lowly. Surely there must be more to her than that! Humility, obedience and lowliness are clearly facets of Mary's character and are supremely significant human attributes. To see more of these attributes would mean living in a much better world today. For me, Mary stands for all these and much more too, although for a long time I wasn't sure what this 'much more' was.

For years I have also felt a kind of personal fascination with the figure of Mary. For a while I was unable to put this into coherent words—I simply felt drawn to her place in the Gospels. Gradually I realised that it was less a fascination and more a quest—a journey to discover who or what this woman really was.

So as I set out on this journey, I feel excited. In many ways I feel a sense of release that at last I now have the opportunity to combat some of the negativity around. My hope for this book is to show that Mary cannot be the private property of a few selected Christian traditions—she lies at the heart of what the gospel truly is for all believers. I also want to show that she was far more than a loving mother to a 'gentle Jesus', by looking at powerful and radical ways Mary witnesses to the grace of a life transfigured. The annunciation transfigured her; watching her son's behaviour transfigured her; being presented to 'another' at the foot of the cross transfigured her and being with the other disciples after the resurrection transfigured her. The grace of transfiguration was not a private gift to those who accompanied Jesus up a high mountain. The 'glimpse of the eternal' that they caught that day was a promise that transfiguration was a gift to all people—and in her life Mary shows that to be true and freely given.

Then I want to explore the ways in which my initial fascination with what Mary was as a human being became a journey of discovery. I want to explore the ways in which so many people are drawn to Mary as a historical figure of human liberation. Here we encounter a woman, a confused woman who encountered God, a humiliated woman who came to terms with scorn, a young woman who coped with a steep learning curve, a frightened woman who took a risk, a mournful woman who discovered transfiguration. In a sense she is presented almost as a figure of disgrace—young, pregnant, potentially rejected by Joseph, at the receiving end of her father's wrath, even risking death by stoning.

One of the more interesting contemporary portrayals of the human Mary was in Tony Jordan's production of the TV series *The Nativity*. I was drawn to the way in which he conveyed both the shepherds—particularly one called Thomas—and Mary. In a BBC news presentation in December 2010, he said, 'The problem is that everyone that exists in the story of the nativity is a cardboard cut-out... Who were they? Why was it important for them to be there?' These two questions will weave their way throughout my exploration of Mary: who was she? Why was it important for her to be there? I want to show that both the Gospel portrayal of Mary and our contemporary experience of Mary are anything but 'cardboard cut-outs'.

Moving on an exciting journey

To map my way through this exciting journey, I have adopted a somewhat novel approach. I take as my overarching structure the Gospel experience of transfiguration, because of all the Gospel experiences, I feel that the events up that high mountain, recorded in the Gospels of Matthew, Mark and Luke, are one experience in the ministry of Jesus of which people today can more easily make sense. From the growing interest in relationship dynamics, lifestyle coaching and so on, people generally know what it's like to be changed, to be transformed, to be altered, to be repaired and to move on in a new and transfigured way—it is about making peace with the past before it is too late. Throughout her life Mary moved in a way that shows she lived a life transfigured; her life was one of startling interruptions, yet through her experience of transfiguration she was able to move on. It is at this point that we discover a vital resonance between Mary and so many people in our own day.

For Mary, as for many others throughout the ages, 'moving on' to live a life transfigured was an experience of liberation. In mapping my way through this journey, I use a way of reflecting theologically which is called the 'liberation method'. Essentially this way of 'doing' theology is based on two precepts. Firstly, it is based on firm biblical foundations. On the one hand, the Christian belief in the doctrine of the incarnation provides the basis for insisting that we must start our theologising from our own real situations within the life of this world. We must be incarnational in our approach. It is in this world that God has been at work and still is at work. History is the place of encounter between God and human beings; salvation comes to us within the boundaries of history. On the other hand, the Exodus story in the Old Testament portrays a God who liberated the oppressed and his great act of deliverance is an act of political human liberation. The Israelites were delivered from a state of actual political subjection and, as a result of their release, they eventually became a nation in their own right, a political entity. This act of liberation is all of a piece with the whole of God's activity throughout human history, because the original act of creation was itself an act of deliverance—deliverance from chaos. In the New Testament we find that the work of Christ also results in a new creation and is the supreme means of liberation. At the same time, this supreme act of deliverance is basically the continuation and culmination of the divine process of liberation stretching back to the very start of Genesis.

Set my people free

Secondly, this way of reflecting theologically is based firmly on the biblical witness that God wants to set his people free. The actual term 'liberation theology' has come into use to describe the response of various theologians to contemporary situations of oppression, prejudice and injustice. They insist that the theologian must begin thinking within his or her real life circumstances in the real world, just as the previously mentioned incarnational approach argues. They insist also that the theologian is committed to action as well as to thought, and that this commitment means taking sides with those who are struggling to free the oppressed. The liberation method of 'doing theology' is therefore primarily concerned with applying biblical insights and Christian traditions to real life situations, and provides doctrinal backing for those who seek a different and fairer world.

My study of Mary is thus rooted in a process of liberation which seeks to show how Mary's life is itself a story of liberation—and such liberation applies not only to her life but to ours too. And from liberation comes the real possibility of living transfigured lives. I want to recognise Mary as a human being first—a person who was both a centre of history and a revelation of the divine, as all humans potentially are. Having said this, I will not be setting up two competing histories—one 'divine' and one 'human'. My starting point means recognising one single human history—the scene of conflicts, of joys and of sorrows. The Word becomes flesh in human flesh, historical flesh marked by space and time, life and death, joy and sorrow, building and destroying. It means that we recognise Mary as a historical figure rather than making her an eternal, unchanging model. We must think of her in dialogue with the time, space, culture, problems and actual people who related to her. It is life today that gives life to Mary's life yesterday.

Once I have explored these themes of transfiguration and liberation, my journey towards Mary will continue by exploring various parts of her life, considering how she, as a woman, revealed the real possibility of liberation and how she, as a woman, constantly sought a transfigured life. By exploring the biblical texts about her life, I will reflect on her as a woman standing on the threshold of a transfigured life. By exploring aspects of her human life—mother, partner, disciple—I will reflect on her as a woman emerging as a sign of the liberating kingdom of God. By exploring her life in Nazareth and her anguish at the foot of the cross, I will reflect on her as a woman bearing the incarnation and witnessing the resurrection. Finally, by exploring the ways her story challenges us to see Christ anew, I will show how this woman testifies to God's continuing power of transfiguration in our lives today.

Part 1

Threshold of transfiguration

It might appear a bit strange to start a book on Mary by referring directly to the events surrounding the transfiguration of Jesus. That day Jesus shared with Peter, James and John at the top of a high mountain must have been an amazing experience. Although the Gospels of Matthew, Mark and Luke vary on some of the detail, all three place the event at a 'threshold' moment in the unfolding of Jesus' ministry. In Matthew's Gospel (17:1–13) it happens between the first prediction of the passion of Jesus, with crucially important words on what it truly means to be a disciple (16:24–26), and the second prediction, in which Jesus spells out clearly that his death is imminent (17:22–23). Similarly in Mark (9:2–8) the event happens between those same two predictions concerning the passion but Mark presents the experience as an anticipation of the final coming of God's kingdom. The meaning of discipleship and the closeness of God's kingdom are also the context of Luke's account of the transfiguration (9:28–36).

This 'threshold' theme of the transfiguration also comes out in the way in which we as readers of the Gospels are encouraged to look back and to look forward. On the mountain, images and themes are used which force us to look back at the story as it has unfolded, but with a different kind of vision. The disciples had until that point fumbled around, failing to realise who Jesus was; now they were dazzled by the truth. It also points us forward—the same triad, Peter, James and John, will once again take centre-stage in Gethsemane. The transfiguration, then, is the pivot on which the whole life and ministry of Jesus turns. Interestingly, Mark points out that the significance of the transfiguration cannot be fully understood until after the resurrection (9:9). Luke suggests the same thing when he states that the conversation between Jesus, Moses and Elijah on the mountain was the 'exodus' that Jesus was about to accomplish in Jerusalem (9:31).

This threshold moment in the Gospel narratives, when 'the penny began to drop' for the disciples, comes mid-point in Jesus' ministry—between a period of introducing the news of God's kingdom and the final journey to the cross. For me the key to grasping the full meaning of the transfiguration is its connection with the cross. Peter, James and John caught a glimpse that day of the glory of God as it was unfolding before their eyes and as such it prepared them for making eventual sense of what lay ahead.

Looking God straight in the eye

The whole experience of transfiguration, then, points us to the intrinsic connection between suffering and glory, and how suffering can be transcended. Transfiguration always prefigures resurrection and shows how life is lived in tension between the visible and the invisible, between anticipation and fulfilment. Again, it is significant that both Matthew and Mark show Jesus charging his disciples to tell no one what they had seen until after the Son of Man was raised from the dead. It is always only in the light of the resurrection that others will be able to draw close to him, to gaze upon him and to draw inspiration from his transfiguring power.

Many of the early Christian writers, building upon the events of the New Testament, highlighted the transfiguration as an experience that people generally could share in and understand. They argued that the transfiguration of Jesus would not be complete until, as a way of life, it was fully embraced by Christians seeking to live out the good news in their own era. One of the profoundest biblical insights about transfiguration is that, when we look at the transfigured Christ, we ourselves are changed—transfigured—in order to become the means by which others can come to share in this new way of living. Those early Christians who were writing about the transfiguration soon after the New Testament period were less keen to talk of it in terms of an event on a mountain in Palestine and more as an experience still freely available today.

Accordingly, Irenaeus of Lyons (c. 130–c. 200) was right to say that, for him, the glory of God is always revealed in a human life being lived to the full, which in turn shows that human life in tune with the vision of God. Similarly, John of Damascene (c. 675–749) said, 'Christ is transfigured not by putting on some quality he did not possess previously, nor by changing into something he never was before, but by revealing to his disciples what he truly was, in opening their eyes and in giving sight to those who were blind' (*Liber de Haeresibus*, 80).

There is a tradition in the scriptures that human beings cannot look upon the face of God (see, for example, Genesis 32:30; Exodus 33:22–23; Judges 6:22). The transfiguration of Jesus turns this tradition on its head and actually enables humans to gaze upon the face of God, but always with the proviso that they do it in the knowledge that they themselves will be changed. Indeed, it may well be that this willingness to be changed becomes a kind of condition upon which we are able to look at God fully. In *The Dwelling of the Light* (Canterbury Press, 2003), a book on one of the icons of the transfiguration, Rowan Williams writes: 'Looking at Jesus seriously changes things; if we do not want to be changed, it is better not to look too hard or too long.' The transfiguration offers a glimpse of the inner dimension of the life of Jesus—the hidden glory—but it also offers a way for men and women to live with courage a life open to the heights and depths from which Jesus lived. Again, Rowan Williams writes: 'Knowing that Christ is in the heart of darkness, we are called to go there with him—but if we have seen his glory on the mountain, we know at least that death cannot decide the boundaries of God's life.' To capture all of this, the Orthodox Church has a doctrine they call *theosis*, which affirms that human beings can actually be partakers of the divine nature. God became human, so that humans might become God; it is by the action of God that it is possible for these two mysteries to take place. It is by the action of God that these mysteries also enter time and space in Christ and in the life of all who belong to Christ.

Much non-biblical religious literature also captures the sense in which *theosis* makes it possible to enter into the transfigured life. Poets, for instance, can show the way in which the disciples on the mountain experienced a special revelation about the nature of Christ—it was not that Christ himself changed in this moment. Rather, it was the disciples who were given the grace to see him anew. R.S. Thomas (1913–2000) alludes to the power of transfiguration in his sonnet 'The Bright Field'. Although a poem referring specifically to the parable of the treasure hidden in a field and the pearl of great price (Matthew 13:44–46), his references to Moses and to a 'brightness' that seems transitory but is eternal, evoke the story of the transfiguration. The poem that I find particularly powerful in relation to all of this is the one by a Spanish poet Miguel de Unamuno (1864–1936). In 'The Christ of Velazquez' he refers to the bright cloud that covered Jesus on the mountain as a metaphor for Christ himself.

A white cloud you are, white as the one
that across the desert guided
the children of Israel...

The American poet e.e. cummings (1894–1962) strikes a powerful note when he says that the world was transfigured for him when 'the eyes of my eyes were opened' and he thanks God for that moment of pure transfiguration. What a contrast to Peter's situation on the mountain with Jesus! He too must have felt something like the euphoria expressed by cummings. However, Jesus did not allow his followers to rest in ecstatic bliss—they had to descend to the plain and deal with the other disciples' botched attempt at healing (Matthew 17:14–21). As always in transfiguration the moment of vision is not given for its own sake, but it demands a response—in this case, of discipleship. The mountain top experience is not an exclusive affair nor a private spiritual high for the privileged few, but a converting experience for all those on the plains who believe in his power to transform, to breathe new life into what is lifeless.

Mary in the human and divine the drama

Where does Mary fit? I'm convinced that Mary and the events surrounding the transfiguration are connected at two levels—a human one and the divine one. The first level places Mary in a very human place as a woman who was transformed and ultimately transfigured herself. Arguably, just like her son, Mary was troubled by contradictions in her understanding of the will of God. According to Luke, whose report quite possibly includes the original transfiguration tradition, Jesus resolved his difficulties in prayer and then his face shone. The glory that Peter, James and John saw (Luke 9:32) was perhaps the radiant joy that accompanies the resolution of a terrible perplexity. On at least two occasions Mary was also caught up in perplexity: first by the presence of an angel telling her about a strange and unexpected pregnancy (Luke 1:26–38), and second at the foot of the cross as she gazed into the eyes of her own suffering and dying son (John 19:25). The grace of transfiguration is seen in her as she comes to terms with both these times of baffling perplexity. At the annunciation, grace was revealed as she sang her hymn of exultation (Luke 1:46–55) and at the cross grace was revealed as her dying son presents her to John's care (John 19:25–27)—precious moments indeed. But notice that, as she is presented to John, Jesus uses the unusual term 'woman', suggesting maybe that the evangelist sees more in this act of presentation than merely the gesture of a dutiful son. With that word 'woman', this could be read as a declaration that Mary is the new Eve, the spiritual mother of all God's faithful people. We will reflect more on this title later.

The second level at which Mary connects with the events of the transfiguration brings us to a divine place. The central affirmation of the Christian faith declares that God himself has entered into our human situation and in doing so has totally transfigured it. In the early Christian centuries this affirmation was expressed succinctly by Athanasius (Bishop of Alexandria in 328): 'God became man so that man might become God.' Such a statement necessarily implies that the Christian gospel can only fit into a radically transfigured world. It means a revolution not only of our idea of God but also of our idea of humanity and of the world in which we live. This brings us right back to the Orthodox understanding of the process of *theosis*—our gradually becoming partakers of the divine nature through God's transfiguring grace. As a process it is inseparably and necessarily bound up with the incarnation of God in the person of Jesus Christ—both an event and an experience directly related to the life of Mary.

I'm quite certain that over the generations many of our misunderstandings concerning Jesus stem from an inadequate understanding of God. Corresponding to this inadequate vision of God stands an inadequate vision of our human nature. Such an inadequacy means that as men and women we have somehow lost our original vision that human beings were in fact created in order to achieve full union with God, to be capable to be the actual place of God's presence. Without this process of *theosis* there is a real danger that incarnation loses its meaning. For how can God enter into humanity unless human beings are made from the beginning to enter into God?

The explicit affirmation that we are made partakers of the divine nature occurs only once in the New Testament (2 Peter 1:4). But the Pauline teaching about our incorporation into Christ through the work of the Holy Spirit and John's teaching about the human/divine indwelling both affirm a relation of unlimited intimacy with God. Throughout the New Testament the human and divine indwelling implies a relationship of both union and communion which overthrows worldly ways of thinking about God's relationship with humanity and that we are miserable sinners, unworthy of his attention. It opens the way towards the wonder of our adoption into the life of God. If this is so for humanity generally, then Mary as the bearer of the incarnation—the one who at a particular moment in history responded positively to God, thus making it all happen—must surely occupy a central role in the process of *theosis* as well as the grace of transfiguration.

As we explore the scriptural portrayal of Mary as a woman liberated and transfigured, we can recognise her as one who offers hope and the opportunity of a life transfigured to those who, from whatever context, cry for freedom. We also need to recognise that this calls for a different and special way of reading the biblical texts. The written evidence for Mary's life must always make us wonder what was not recorded or never made it to the canonical collection of texts. What was lost and what was left out on purpose? A written text is always selective and the scriptures that speak about Mary are scarce, but from them and from a variety of early non-biblical material and traditions, each historical era has constructed a different image of Mary and her historical activity. Hence it is not possible to say that the only truth about Mary's life is in the little that we are told by the early Christian writers. What is not said is also important.

Chapter 1

Songs and cries of Hebrew children

In his book *Mary through the Centuries* (Yale University Press, 1996) the American theologian Jaroslav Pelikan reminds us of the way in which some biblical interpreters use the idea of the hiddenness of the New Testament in the Old and the Old Testament becoming visible in the New to highlight the unity of the whole of the Bible. For Christian interpreters it means moving comfortably from one Testament to another and, by so doing, highlighting that move from prophecy to fulfilment. For some people, a first reading of the Gospels is probably surprising as they are struck that so little is said about Mary, so this idea of being able to move from one Testament to another is helpful. In reality, in order to construct as big a picture of Mary as possible it is essential to move from Testament to Testament but we need to do even more than that. We need to be ready to move from the Testaments and useful non-scriptural texts into the Jewish world that Mary inherited and occupied. This is what I meant in the introduction by saying that it is in fact not possible to limit what we know about Mary to the little we are told by the early Christian writers. What is not told by them is also crucial. To grasp the real Mary, we need to journey into the world in which she lived as a daughter, a mother and a wife. It was a world saturated with religious enthusiasm and vitality, and the scriptures that she heard in the synagogue, and the rituals and traditions she practised, are crucial to understanding Mary.

Hints of Mary in the Old Testament

And so it is that the Old Testament is my obvious starting point, where typology and allegory play an important role in revealing the full extent of prophecy in the Old being fulfilled in the New—and Mary's role in all of this. Starting in this way helps us to catch glimpses of Mary foreshadowed in the Old Testament. As God prepared the way for Christ throughout the Jewish tradition, so I think the same can be said for Mary. The Roman Catholic biblical scholar Raymond Brown makes the point strongly that the whole history of Israel prepared the way for both Jesus and his mother. He adds that many of the early Church Fathers both in the East and in the West also recognised this kind of foreshadowing (*Mary in the New Testament*, Fortress Press, 1978).

We already know that the Gospel writers were also eager to preserve this connection with the Old Testament—or rather for them, the scriptures (as at that time the New Testament was not written, but being brought to life). From the very beginning, the Christian tradition excitedly proclaimed that Jesus came from the line of David and the root of Jesse. Interestingly, this referred to Joseph rather than Mary—it was Joseph's genealogy, not Mary's, that Matthew and Luke were keen to preserve. However, as Jaroslav Pelikan states, it is those same two evangelists who emphasise Mary's virginity, and so for me the implication is that Jesus' supposed human father was actually less important than Mary. This stress on the lineage of David is in fact an affirmation of Jesus' continuity with the whole history of Israel. If that is so, then Jesus' actual descent had to be through his only human parent, Mary—so in reality isn't she the one that stands in this line of David?

In this chapter I want to explore these Old Testament roots that parallel the life of Mary. I also want to take a sideways move from the Old Testament and journey into some aspects of the Jewish religious world during Mary's lifetime to create a context for her. Then in Chapter 2 I will explore the New Testament evidence.

God's little people

Some years ago I came across the writings of the Roman Catholic theologian Hans Urs von Balthasar—I think it was his name that first attracted me! One of his books drew my attention to the importance of the potentially ambiguous Hebrew word *anawim* which, roughly translated, could mean 'the little people' (literally, 'the oppressed ones'). What fascinated me was Balthasar's relating of this word to the Old Testament proclamation of the ultimate coming of the Messiah—a coming that would establish divine justice and God's grace on earth (*The Glory of the Lord,* vol. 7, T & T Clark, 1989). For the Jewish people at that time such a coming would have been recognised as an act of liberation dramatically affecting those with no rights, those who could not help themselves and the oppressed. By implication, then, this liberation would inevitably move 'the little people' on to centre stage. The prophets (particularly Amos and Isaiah) constantly bemoaned the poverty of the people they ministered to and condemned the governments of the day for shamelessly and openly exploiting the poverty of those people. For them it was a scandal of economics as well as a marring of ethics and as such a serious scar on the relationship between God and his people.

Job, for instance, describes how the poor are naked and hungry at night, and he compares them to animals in the fields and vineyards scratching around for waste food thrown out by their thieving masters (Job 24:2–12). Similarly, the teachers in the wisdom tradition warn against turning away from the poor lest the rich suffer the same fate (Sirach 4:5). If God's justice is incarnated in his people, then there can be no place for hypocrisy on the part of the rich; there is an urgency about facing up honestly to poverty. The prophets also warn that God will take action on behalf of the poor and will eventually bring down the haughty and the proud—for them it is not a question of 'if' but of 'when'. In his ministry among the poor and the oppressed Zephaniah actually categorises poverty as a theological concept in the sense of being humble (Zephaniah 2:3). He tells the people to seek righteousness and humility because by doing so they will gain God's favour on the day of judgement (3:11–13). Here are the roots of God's preferring to side with the poor.

Jeremiah takes this a step further and, as one who knew persecution, ridicule and humiliation at first hand, he names himself a beggar and offers the people a visible sign of God's favour towards the poor and the oppressed (Jeremiah 20:7–18). Isaiah is certain that, although God dwells in the highest heaven, he is close to the humble and to the contrite (Isaiah 57:15; 66:2). Even in the deprivation and poverty of exile those who suffer become the recipients of God's mercy (40:2; 51:3,8; 53:11).

What emerges here is a prophetic portrayal of those who are physically poor and weak, and those who confess their spiritual poverty before God, as the recipients of God's favour and righteousness—these are the true *anawim*. Several of the Psalms recognise this and some of the prayers of the *anawim* are preserved (Psalms 9; 10; 25; 34; 37)—prayers that link humiliation and poverty with victory and righteousness. These Psalms show that the *anawim* recognised God's blessing upon them and that they held on to the hope of God's ultimate salvation (Psalm 149:4–5). The lower the *anawim* bow before God, the higher they triumph over their oppressors, and in understanding this as a call to a life of grace, stripped of material possessions and given back to God, the *anawim* emerge as a distinct group. Bowing in humility become their hallmark (Psalm 40; Proverbs 15:33; 18:12; 22:4) and in doing so their hope remains that God will graciously respond to them. In turn, they respond with gratitude (Baruch 2:18).

Anawim—the roots of the family of Jesus

For me, it is here that we begin to trace the roots of Jesus' family and his whole outlook on life—his philosophy, if you like. These roots help us to begin making sense of Mary's hymn of praise (Luke 1:46–55), the Sermon on the Mount (Matthew 5—7), even Jesus' constant rebuke of Pharisaic hypocrisy (see, for example, Matthew 6; 23; Mark 7). It is in this *anawim* tradition that we can root the idea of the son of David emerging from a humble and ordinary family, thus bearing out the destiny of *anawim* suffering running through the Old Testament. This can also be taken a step further, because the *anawim* actually become the physical bearers of God's presence—in their tribulations, particularly in exile, they stood as a 'waiting people'. Receptively and patiently they waited for God's word, and one of the enduring themes of the Bible is that God prefers the company of those who are badly treated because he himself is constantly let down by those who make false and empty promises of faithfulness. God's children then are always a 'hidden people' in the same way as the *anawim* were hidden from all earthly glories but always remained receptive to God in and through their poverty and sufferings. Such suffering provides God with a ready access to his people and, knowing this to be true, the *anawim* remain particularly open to him and are constantly dependent upon his grace—and their response to him is always a 'yes'!

The Old Testament prophetic tradition is an almost constant commentary on a certain people's experience of being blessed and purified. The harsh bearing of suffering served as a form of purification and in turn established a new and radical spiritual experience. This is Mary's context—a humble virgin from downtown Nazareth becoming the locus of God's glory in the world. The ancient longings of the *anawim* and the promises of the prophets all converge in what God called Mary to become. The *anawim* waited patiently and in their sufferings praised God's word; Mary responded openly and in her purity bore God's Word. For me it goes further still: the true beauty of the *anawim* concept lies in the fact that they were real human beings—not angels, not saints, not special, but ordinary people living day-to-day lives of struggle and worry. Throughout the Judeo-Christian tradition—and especially as revealed in the Bible—the powerful spirit of God keeps pushing ordinary people to become open and vulnerable in order to provide fertile ground for his grace. Is it not arguably the case that one of the climaxes of the whole Gospel narrative is when an ordinary young girl from Nazareth is invited to embody the destiny of God's children by saying 'yes' to him? Rowan Williams captures this powerfully in a sermon when he states that by saying 'yes' to God, Mary enabled a new human life, beginning in her body, to become 'a life in which God's Word is indeed set free, given space to work in the world and make it new... the child she brings forth is an embodiment of creative holiness, the Word made flesh' (*Open to Judgement*, DLT, 1994).

In Mary's 'yes' all the hopes of the *anawim*, which made God's eventual incarnation possible, come to a climax. And it is in this sense that Rowan Williams, in the same sermon, is able to regard Mary as the new ark of the covenant, carrying within herself the sign and seal of God's presence that through her was being returned to his children. The language used by Luke to describe Mary as the bearer of the incarnation is very reminiscent of that used to describe the carrying of the original ark of the covenant to Israel (11 Samuel 6). This is not the only occasion when Mary is seen as either fulfilling previous events or renewing particular experiences recorded in the Old Testament, and this is where typology and allegory come to play a part.

Restoring a lost promise

Over the generations the Church has used several titles to describe Mary. One of the more interesting of these titles was one used in the early days of the Church, describing Mary as the new Eve. Two prominent theologians working in Rome during the second century, Justin Martyr and Irenaeus, used this title in direct reference to Mary. In doing so they inferred that just as the serpent had defeated Eve, so Mary defeats the devil by enabling the Son of God to enter the world as both Lord and Saviour. In other words, what we have here is a counterbalance between the disobedience of Eve in the garden of Eden (Genesis 3) and the obedience of Mary when she said 'yes' to the angel Gabriel (Luke 1:38). Her 'yes' became crucial to the whole experience of the incarnation.

Roman Catholic teaching concerning Mary claims that Eve had been dealt a kind of double death by the serpent, that of sin and that of bodily corruption. The Catholic dogma of the immaculate conception states that Mary was exempt from sin and the dogma of the assumption exempts her from bodily corruption. It is by virtue of this double exemption that Mary is still referred to as the new Eve. Whatever we make of such dogmas, it is interesting that in such teaching the link between Mary and Eve is preserved.

However, as a title for Mary I find 'new Eve' interesting in a slightly different way, because what strikes me is the biblical contrast between Eve and Mary. As through Eve humanity experiences the beginnings of disobedience and crisis, at a moment when all seems lost and beyond hope, so through Mary a new way through despair is gifted. In Mary a lost promise is restored and through the message of an angel the process of disobedience that began with Eve is transfigured—it is more than simply a restoration. When transfiguration occurs, it is always more than what is humanly expected. More than restoring something, more than fulfilling something, it is always an experience of God taking us that one step further. In Mary's 'yes' we encounter a moment that changes the whole direction and significance of the oppression of the *anawim*. They expected liberation from physical slavery, but in Mary's 'yes', and in what happened as a result of her 'yes', humanity was taken a step beyond what was ever thought possible. It is a moment in which eternity and time come together and it establishes complete human and divine reconciliation. In Mary's 'yes' all is potentially restored and regained—transfigured beyond all expectations so that hopelessness is completely reversed.

Two women give thanks for the gift of life

The processes of deciding which books were to make up the final version of the Old and New Testaments were complex. Archaeology and history have shown us that a number of other documents written at about the same time as those contained in the New Testament were left out. Several of these now make up what is known as the New Testament Apocrypha, and one of those books was the so-called Gospel of James (the *Protoevangelium*), which tells the story of Mary's early life in ways that actually resonate with the life of Christ in Luke's Gospel. And Mary's mother Anne in the Gospel of James is closely modelled on the figure of Hannah from the first book of Samuel.

The first book of Samuel opens with a portrayal of the classic oppressed woman who is barren and childless and scorned by her rival within the household—another typical example of the *anawim*. The overall thrust of the story is that Samuel is simply a gift from God to this oppressed woman, and his life is in turn given back to God as a thank-offering (see 1 Samuel 1). To an oppressed Israel under serious Philistine threat, the figure of Samuel is heavily laden with significant hopes for the future—hence the song of Hannah (1 Samuel 2:1–10). Hannah exults in the Lord and rejoices in his salvation. God remains the central figure of her song—none is as holy, none is as protective, none is as hopeful as

God. Hannah, one of the *anawim*, is constantly faithful and characteristically grateful.

Luke tells us that, after the annunciation to Mary and during her pregnancy, she stayed for about three months with her cousin Elizabeth (Luke 1:56). One can almost feel the excitement between the two women but also their fear and awe—hence the song of Mary (Luke 1:46–55). Like Hannah a thousand years before, Mary exults in the Lord and rejoices in his salvation. Again, God is the central figure of her song. Hannah's song was fulfilled in the ministry of Samuel; Mary's song was fulfilled in the ministry of Jesus. Significantly, both Hannah and Mary are members of the *anawim* and in them prophecy and fulfilment come together.

Yet another woman's song of triumph

The Book of Judges is concerned with the period between the death of Joshua and the rise of Saul. The death of Joshua signalled that the age dominated by Moses had finally come to an end. With the rise of Saul, the age of David and the kings begins to take shape. It is a transition that occurs at a time of great danger and uncertainty. Israel finds itself at a threshold but will need help to make the actual transition and to cross that threshold. Great questions are being asked: how do the followers of the old ways—the Canaanites—react to the innovators of the new ways—the Israelites? How will the Israelites interact with different groups of people? How will the people maintain their relationship with God? What will become of the *anawim*? These are just some of the questions that shape the Book of Judges.

Deborah, a judge and a prophetess, plays a significant role in this process of transition from the old to the new—

she was a woman of strength and a great leader. As a Judge she would have been both concerned with and responsible for seeking unity and reconciliation, and as such her moral authority was inspired by God. When her story opens, she is described as habitually seated under a tree between Bethel and Ramah, north of Jerusalem, where the people came to meet her. At the time the Israelites were suffering serious oppression at the hands of the Canaanites. Commanded by God, Deborah comes to the rescue and her song indicates the way in which her call for unity and faithfulness saved the day (Judges 5).

Again, there are significant similarities between the story of Deborah and the story of Mary—both were women, both said 'yes' to God, both sang a song of triumph, and both sang in actual places that were located geographically close to each other. However, what is particularly interesting is that both women found themselves doing God's work at moments of significant transition—between the old and the new.

Mary's world

One of the best ways to understand what the Old Testament truly means to a Jew is to be invited to a Jewish home on a Friday night to share in their celebration of the sabbath. For Jews the sabbath itself is 'the Queen' and the Friday evening celebration marks the arrival of 'the Queen' both into that home and into the lives of those who celebrate together. For Jews the home is regarded as a sanctuary—theologically as important even as the synagogue itself—and, as in a synagogue or a place of public worship, various household furnishings acquire religious significance. On the Friday evening the dining room table becomes the altar, the normal white tablecloths become the drapes on which the sacred vessels and ornaments rest—candlesticks, carefully plaited bread and some wine. It is the woman, the mother, who makes the first move by lighting the candle and reciting a prayer to mark the start of the ceremonies. When this has happened, the father pronounces a blessing on the gathering using the words of Numbers 6:24–26 and, as soon as the celebration gets going, the man turns to the woman and 'sings a song', either literally or simply reciting the words. The song is the one that ends the book of Proverbs (31:10–31) in which wives and mothers and by implication women generally are revered in the biblical tradition. Is such reverence a true reflection of women at the time of Mary? What was a woman's position in the home? What was it like for Mary, living and worshipping at that time? Was she in fact a member of the *anawim* simply by virtue of her gender?

Judaism at that time was full of rules and regulations. Then, as today, the mark of a good Jew was a willingness to follow these commandments—a typical Gentile mistake is to think that there are only ten of them! In fact, the traditional calculation states that there are 613 commandments—365 of them prohibitions and 248 positive commands. The study of these commandments has always been regarded as an integral part of Jewish life and education. Generally speaking, the main thrust of religious laws found in the Old Testament allowed very little space for female manoeuvring with hardly any independence and quite heavy male domination. Unmarried women remained the property of their fathers, a property that was passed to the husband upon marriage, although the world into which Mary was born had in fact improved in this respect.

Young girls over twelve were no longer considered to be property; they kept their income and could even choose husbands. Within the marriage relationship a good degree of security had been introduced by the time Mary was connected to Joseph. Husbands were legally obliged to respect and support their wives, and specific contracts were drawn up at the time of marriage. Such contracts were known as *ketubah*, and they were not simply evidence of marriage but an accurate record of the bride's rights in the event of the husband's death or his divorcing her. The *Mishnah* (the religious law transmitted orally to Moses and not recorded in the Bible), the Babylonian and Palestinian Talmuds (collections of additional ancient legal reports) and the *Tosefta* (additions to the *Mishnah*) all provide valuable information regarding the laws and regulations to do with marriage, and also what life was actually like for women.

By the time of Mary's pregnancy a man could easily divorce his wife but the opposite was not possible. Interestingly, though, if both husband and wife sought to divorce, then that was extremely straightforward—it only needed the presence of two witnesses and not even a court. A court case would certainly have been involved if either husband or wife contested the divorce, where the precise meaning of Deuteronomy 24:1–4 would have been debated. Such a debate can be detected in Matthew 19:1–12 when Jesus is challenged by the Pharisees to express his views on the law of Deuteronomy. Jesus seems to suggest that unfaithfulness is the only grounds for divorce. This helps us to understand Matthew 1:19 a little better, when, on hearing about Mary's pregnancy, Joseph does seem to consider divorce as an option—probably on the supposed basis that she had been unfaithful to him. At that time an engagement in Jewish law was as binding as marriage but in an engagement the couple did not live in the same house. Quite possibly, Joseph's dilemma was whether to take the matter before a court, thus making the news public, or whether to secure a private divorce. The Gospels record that thoughts of divorce were short-lived for Joseph, and he decided to support Mary (see Matthew 1:19:–24).

One of the other major laws affecting women in Mary's situation was that of ritual uncleanness, during menstruation (Leviticus 15:19–24) and following childbirth (12:2–8). Such uncleanness meant that the woman concerned could not enter the temple or participate in certain acts of worship. However, remedies were at hand once the prescribed time of waiting had passed—seven days for menstruation and, following childbirth, seven days if the child was male and 14 if she was a girl. On the eighth day the boy was circumcised but the mother had to await a purification for a further 33 days. At the end of the waiting time she offered two sacrifices—a ram as a whole offering and a turtle dove as a sin offering.

The Gospel of Luke describes some of these rituals, and we read that Jesus was indeed circumcised on the eighth day (2:21) and, like all other Jewish boys at that time, he received his name at the same ceremony. Then when the time was right, Mary went to the temple to complete the process of her purification from uncleanness and offered the necessary sacrifices (v. 22). It seems that they were not particularly wealthy people because they gave two pigeons instead of the prescribed ram—an acceptable legal option for the *anawim*.

Less segregation

Today, public worship can take place in an orthodox Jewish synagogue only if at least ten adult Jewish males are present. Women do not qualify as part of this quorum. Furthermore, women are separated from men within the synagogue—women worship in an *ezrat nashim*, a balcony or a section set apart. A former teacher of mine in Jerusalem, whose work I have found particularly helpful in trying to reconstruct the kind of world Mary inhabited, is Shmuel Safrai. He has always been convinced that things could well have been considerably different (men and women were not segregated) in the synagogue in Nazareth in which Mary and Jesus worshipped (*The Land of Israel and its Sages in the Mishnaic and Talmudic Period*, United Kibbutz Publishing Co., 1983).

In the first century and earlier, it seems that women were quite possibly the equals of men as far as worship in the synagogue was concerned, and they visited it frequently. This is demonstrated by a verse in the book of Judges, where it is recorded that Deborah blesses Jael, who is described as 'most blessed of women' (5:24). From earliest times Jews have been extremely careful in their interpretation of the scriptures. Endless studies of words and phrases in order to achieve an accurate meaning have occupied Jewish scholars for generations and one such tradition of scholarship is contained in the Targums—translations of the Hebrew text of the Old Testament into Aramaic. There is one such Targum that translates Judges 5:24 to the effect that Jael was 'like one of the women who attend the houses of study and she will be blessed'. It translates 'tents' as 'house of study' (in Hebrew the word is *Bet Midrash*), which is an equivalent expression for synagogue.

Similarly, in the Jerusalem Talmud the hypothetical question is raised: in a town in which all the residents are priests, when they spread their hands in the synagogue and give their priestly blessing, who responds 'Amen'? (The priests themselves are not permitted to give the response to their own blessing.) The answer is: 'the women and the children'. Women were therefore in attendance in the synagogue, otherwise how could they shout the Amen? In a different Talmud (Babylonian) the following teaching is found: a Jewish woman may set a pot on the stove and let a Gentile woman come and stir its contents until she returns from the synagogue. The implication here is that the synagogue was one of the places to which Jewish women normally went. In one of the minor tracts of the Soferim Talmud an interesting regulation is mentioned: although on sabbaths the people come early to the synagogue, on festivals they come later because they have food to prepare. The second 'they' refers to the female members of the congregations. It was the women who needed the early morning hours of holidays for preparation of food. Much of the preparation of the main holiday meal, eaten at midday after the family returned from the synagogue, was done before they left home. Lighting a fire to cook food, while not permitted on ordinary sabbaths, was permitted on festivals. Therefore, to accommodate the women, the synagogue service started later on festival days. If the women's participation in synagogue worship had been felt to be less vital than that of the men, there would have been no reason to delay the holiday service—the men could have conducted the service while the women were at home, preparing the meal.

The Gospels tell us that Mary and her child visited the temple (Luke 2:41–52) and we should also note that women were allowed in every area of the temple precincts. The women's court, the outer court of the temple, was not reserved exclusively for women; in this court men and women mingled. Men had to pass through the women's court to reach the Israelites' court (men's court) and located in the women's court were various chambers, such as the Nazirites' Chamber, to which both men and women had access. Public assemblies took place in the women's court—it was there that the High Priest read the Torah before the people on the Day of Atonement, as stated in the Babylonian Talmud.

The outer court of the temple was called the women's court because normally women did not go beyond it into the more interior courts. Similarly, the Israelites' court was so named because normally non-priestly men did not go beyond it into the priests' court. However, like men, women offered their sacrifices at the altar in the priests' court, passing through the Israelites' court in order to do so. Women were actually segregated in the temple only during the water-drawing ceremony held on the Feast of Tabernacles, when dancing went on all night. Both the Babylonian Talmud and the Mishnah inform us that at this celebration, men watched from the women's court and women watched from specially erected galleries surrounding the women's court.

Religious opportunities for Mary were not as restricted as life for Jewish women at other times in history may have been. She would have had the space and the freedom to accompany her son in his spiritual nurture—and she could also have played her own part in that spiritual life. After all, she had conversed with an angel!

Theological underpinning

Two important words in this chapter have been 'prophecy' and 'fulfilment': the promises of the Old Testament prophets regarding the coming of God's kingdom, a redeeming Messiah and better times were fulfilled in Christ. A significant term in relation to all this is 'progressive revelation'. As we move from the Old Testament to the New, we find a progressive revelation of God's working his purpose out, which is also at the heart of the life of Mary. Our exploration of only a few Old Testament and Jewish themes and events in this chapter shows that Mary did not simply appear at the right time and in the right place and vanish once her deed was done. God's continuing creative and redeeming love was (and continues to be) revealed progressively and Mary plays a central role in that progression.

Chapter 2

New Testament variations on Mary

In this chapter I don't intend simply to comment on the few New Testament passages that mention Mary, but rather to consider how her life was transfigured and how that life offers signs of liberation. I have already described what I mean by living a transfigured life—a life that is always moving one step beyond transformation and change, in a process of liberation and renewal. Actually recognising transformation or change in one's own life must always precede a state of transfiguration. A transfigured life is what happens thereafter—journeying forward with integrity and having, as it were, a godly spring to your step!

The songs and cries of those Hebrew women mentioned in the previous chapter revealed God's saving power; their resistance to oppression and persecution was an indisputable statement that in God's liberating work his glory also shines. As we have seen, reflecting theologically in a liberation context, we discover the life of Mary not simply as an individual young girl from Nazareth, but rather as one who images a whole faithful listening people—the *anawim*. The statement of faith that proclaims that in Jesus God becomes flesh (John 1:14) always carries with it the knowledge of another equally important theological statement that God was born of a woman (Galatians 4:4–5). The New Testament shows that with Mary Jesus ushers in a new era of history—

this is a massive and radical leap. God now dwells on earth and is discovered and loved in human flesh. Mary's initial role in this massive leap is as the bearer of an equally radical new hope, a new way of being human that was now being offered. We need to ask not only what her story implied over 2000 ago but what that story continues to offer today's *anawim*.

Why such brevity?

I have mentioned several times that the New Testament accounts are surprisingly brief about Mary. Why is such a key player in the whole drama of the incarnation treated almost as a passer-by? Imagine someone who has spent many years as a devotional 'fan' of Mary, travelling to several of the traditional places of pilgrimage associated with her, such as Lourdes and Fatima, then deciding to explore the New Testament record of her life. That person could well end up feeling very disappointed! And if that exploration was to begin by looking her name up in one of the major scholarly lexicons of the New Testament, our 'fan' would be horrified to read that 'little is known about the life of *this* Mary' (William Arndt and Wilbur Ginrich, *A Greek–English Lexicon of the New Testament and other Early Christian Literature*, Chicago University Press, 1957). The contrast between the biblical evidence and traditions surrounding Mary is striking.

The Anglican theologian John Macquarrie, in his book *Mary for all Christians* (T & T Clark, 2001), makes a very helpful point in regard to this brevity. He rightly says that theology cannot possibly be concerned only with the facts of history, only with what is written. Theology is concerned also with how the historical facts have been reflected upon and brought into the body of beliefs concerning the way God has revealed himself in and through history. The task of the theologian is to look at the whole picture—facts, traditions, devotions, spirituality, art—and make a careful inquiry into the process of how beliefs have developed.

Of course, Mary is not the only example of a great contrast between biblical evidence and historical traditions. Perhaps the most decisive example of what could be called the 'development of doctrine' is the church's teaching on the Trinity. The Trinity is not, as such, a New Testament teaching but it has emerged from the life, worship and theological reflection of Christians over many centuries. The church's teaching on the Trinity is in many ways the direct result of generations of careful theological reflection that eventually became a summary of the whole Christian experience of the living God. The same is true about the leap from those simple words of institution uttered by Jesus over supper in the upper room to the resplendent Eucharistic liturgies of the Church throughout the world. But—and this is a big 'but'—a good number of Christians fully accept the development of doctrine concerning the Trinity, yet reject developments in other doctrines, such as those surrounding Mary. It is interesting to ponder why that might be the case, and I intend to do so in the closing chapter.

Paul and Mary

As the letters of Paul are probably the earliest written documents in the New Testament, it is appropriate to begin with him. However, there is only one reference to Mary in the whole of Paul's collection of letters—and he does not even name her! In fairness to Paul, he was not a historian and on the whole he did not concern himself with historical detail. He is less concerned with the facts about the earthly life of Jesus and far more concerned about his own experiences of the risen Christ. Because of this, Paul may not even have known the name of Jesus' earthly mother, but the reference in his letter to the Galatians (4:4–5) to the fact that Jesus had been born of a 'woman' is almost certainly a reference to Mary.

The reference is probably designed to make the point that Jesus was 'one of us', born like us and sharing life in much the same way as we do, and as such he stands in solidarity with us. The figure of the woman who gives birth to the son of God 'in the fullness of time' means the reconciliation between present and future, between things human and things divine—no dualism, no either/or. To reduce the humanity of all this in any way brings us dangerously close to admitting that the Word did not really become flesh in the flesh of men and women. Paul's point is that the kingdom has in fact come in Christ, that the 'fullness of time' has been reached in Christ, that the new creation has become reality in Christ. Why? Because God has sent the Son, born of a woman. In the light of this, the kingdom of God can happen in the community of men and women, whose struggles and sufferings, sorrows and joys constantly blossom with the inexhaustible freshness of love—and that is characteristic of liberation.

Paul's reference to the actual timing of Jesus' birth is also significant, with his memorable phrase the 'fullness of the time' (Galatians 4:4, KJV). In one sense, he is making a historical point, and behind it lies Paul's preoccupation with the careful way God is working out his plans of redemption in the world. Again, this brings us back to the birth of Jesus—a birth that is seen as a moment of climax for Israel initially and the whole world eventually. With that birth, all the longings and waitings of the *anawim* reach a decisive point. What had originated in God (John 1:1) was, in the birth of Jesus, being ushered into the world and through it a new time for the kingdom of God was inaugurated. Subsequently, if God did have a careful plan and if the *anawim* of Israel, since the very beginning of time, were part of that plan, then Mary is a key figure. And, if by 'fullness of time' Paul is in fact referring to a new phase in the unfolding of God's kingdom (as I believe he is), then Mary is a significant link between God's creative and redeeming mission and men and women of this world.

Mark's Mary is a mother... but not a very devoted one

In the chronological scheme of things Mark's Gospel, written about 20 years or so after Paul's ministry to the people of Galatia, comes next. Unlike Paul, Mark did know the name of Jesus' mother but he uses it only once.

The opening of Mark's Gospel has always intrigued me. Imagine for a moment that those people responsible for putting the New Testament together—cutting and pasting the various books and letters—had only one Gospel. Imagine that archaeology had unearthed only Mark's Gospel and that for all sorts of reasons the other Gospels were never found. There would certainly be no celebration of Christmas but maybe baptism, both as an act of initiation and as a covenant relationship that binds Christians to each other and to the risen Christ, would be far more respected than it is in many Christian circles today. Christians might even then remember the dates of their own baptism!

It has often been said that Mark's agenda was simply the plain presentation of the facts as he understood them.

His Mary is a simple mother, and his Gospel contains the barest of references to her; for him her role was simply to 'mother' Jesus into being. He identifies Jesus as a carpenter who knows the law and the prophets, defends the ordinary people, and is accepted by some and rejected by others. Mary shares this context—one that opens and closes horizons, welcomes and rejects Jesus. She stands with those men and women who come close to rejecting him; she even colludes with the group who think Jesus is mad (Mark 3:21)! Because of her willingness to respond to God's invitation to bear his son, she is surely among those who eagerly seek to do God's will—a disciple (v. 35). But she is a mother as a disciple, not a mother and also a disciple. Discipleship is the bigger picture for Mark and it is within discipleship that Mary's role as a mother is defined.

I suspect that the important reference to Mary in Mark's Gospel is in connection with the family home in Nazareth (vv. 20–35). By the time we reach chapter 3, Jesus' campaign is well established and opposition is rife. For whatever reason he returns to the 'safety' of the family home, only to find that even there he is no longer welcome. A crowd turns up and the family meal is spoilt—the setting is tense and Jesus must face up to the consequences of his campaign. Having to deal with an unruly crowd outside is one thing, but this new family conflict and Mark's portrayal of it is interesting. According to Mark, Jesus' own family is now of the opinion that he has gone too far and they want him to give up his mission (v. 21). Their caution comes too late, however, and already Jesus' political and spiritual detractors are on his back (v. 22). And so his ministry in Capernaum ends with a kind of double counterattack upon him—to his extended family he is deluded, to his political and spiritual opponents he is demonic.

There is something very human about this brewing family crisis, which is echoed in some of the other Gospels in different ways. We might well be sympathetic with Mary and the rest of the extended family urgently wanting to silence Jesus. To them it was probably lunacy for a marked man to continue to provoke the highest authorities in the land. He was courting disaster and they wanted to protect him, as well as their family reputation, no doubt! Family life was the major axis of society at this time, but for Mark, this family life is the backbone of the very social order that Jesus is struggling to overturn. Realising this can help us make sense of Mark's utter lack of interest in Jesus' family line (in contrast to Matthew and Luke). It is a strange picture but one that begins to move the reader forward to a much greater rift: Jesus' 'true' family is 'outside' the house (v. 31) and the crowd is inside. Liberation theology recognises here two important questions. Who exactly is 'inside' and who exactly is 'outside'? And what is asked of those who seek to be on the 'inside' of Jesus' new community?

Later on in the same Gospel (6:1–6) Jesus pays another visit to Nazareth and similar tensions arise again. This time the people of his home town are offended at his behaviour—they know the family, so how can he possibly be a teacher? Here the community that has been closest to him for 30 years rejects Jesus' claims. I mentioned earlier that I find the opening of Mark's Gospel intriguing, and the family and home community rifts intrigue me further. Had Mary actually experienced a memory lapse? Had she forgotten what had happened that day in Nazareth when she conversed with an angel? Had 30 years really taken their toll on her and made her forget her own significant theological role in God's acts of salvation? I don't think so! There must surely be more to it than that.

For me it is much more likely that Mark had not in fact heard about those early events. After all, he was writing nearly 20 years or so before Luke had got hold of those more personal details about Mary and the events surrounding her pregnancy. One thing is certain: the details that we do glean from Mark have a ring of reality about them. I, for one, could easily imagine such family tensions and that at times, with the best will in the world, mothers are not always devoted, supportive and encouraging! Difficult times occur in all family circles, without exception.

This process of alienation between Jesus and his family is not one-sided (3:33), however, because if the family cannot support him, then it seems he cannot be part of the family circle. At this stage Mark introduces a new family model that is based on obedience and fidelity to God alone (v. 35), and consists not necessarily of blood relatives. Jesus has already challenged the traditional authority structures of his Palestinian society and now he goes one step further. He has repudiated the old order (2:21) in order to make way for a new one. The fundamental unit of this kingdom order is the new family, which is the community of discipleship. And this new, transfigured order calls for the liberation of the *anawim*.

Matthew prioritises fulfilment

Reading Matthew's Gospel, we should note its focus on the idea of 'fulfilment' and the way in which the evangelist seeks to portray the whole life of Jesus as the fulfilment of all God's promises to his chosen people. At the very beginning of the book of Genesis (1:2) the Spirit (a feminine noun is used) of God hovered over the surface of the waters; at the beginning of Matthew that same Spirit hovers over Mary (1:18) and she gives birth to Jesus. Matthew's picture of Mary is clever; for him Joseph is the synthesis of God's ancient people—a waiting people—eager and ready to recognise the saving Messiah, despite any doubts and difficulties. Mary is the symbol of all faithful people, from whom the saving Messiah is to be born. For Matthew she is a symbol of virgin hope, a woman pregnant with life itself. Joseph is called into a new kind of relationship in order to begin love anew; through Mary God's faithfulness is enabled to re-emerge from the ruins of destruction. As a member of the *anawim*, her 'yes' to God enables her to journey into a transfigured life.

Matthew's picture of Mary is also very God-orientated—he wants to make it plain that Mary's pregnancy and Jesus' birth depend entirely on the initiative of God. Mary's role as the mother of Jesus is closely related to the climax of all that had been promised in the Old Testament. The radical and liberating newness of God's initiative begins in his choice of a girl with no greatness, as the means of bringing about that climax—and this is startling stuff! In this, Matthew presents us with a brand-new world of grace and glory.

In his account of the relationship between Jesus and his mother, Matthew adds new material to what we read in Mark, as, unlike him, Matthew is keen to explore the beginnings of Jesus' earthly life and offers details about his birth and his parents. Like Luke, Matthew dates the birth of Jesus to the reign of Herod the Great, who died about the year 4BC, and so the birth could have occurred some time between the years 6 and 7BC. Matthew also claims that the birth was virginal, and according to him an angel appears to Joseph, who in turn confirms that the pregnancy is all down to God (1:20). Luke, on the other hand, offers a slightly different version of the chain of events and claims that the angel appeared to Mary (Luke 1:31, 35). I intend to return to the virginal conception of Jesus in Chapters 4 and 5, but suffice it to say here that in these claims to a virgin birth, Matthew (as does Luke) gives to Mary a unique and crucial place in God's redeeming work.

Unlike Mark and John, Matthew and Luke also include other details surrounding the birth and childhood of Jesus and it is Matthew who includes the story of the magi and Herod's anger as well as the escape of Jesus, Mary and Joseph to Egypt (2:1–18).

Luke gives new meaning to old beliefs

Here is the Gospel with the most references to Mary. At the start of Luke's presentation of the events surrounding Jesus' birth, what strikes me is the way in which the annunciation to Mary (Luke 1:26–38) is completely in line with the many manifestations of God's faithfulness to his people of old—Sarah and Abraham for instance (see Genesis 12—22). As such, Mary—an authentic representative of all people—is, for Luke, the new ark of the covenant, God's liberating dwelling place and the place where he can be met and loved. Luke uses the experiences and theological expressions of the Hebrew people and gives them new meaning in terms of the transfiguration that can be achieved by Jesus' followers. Mary's visit to Elizabeth (Luke 1:39–45), for instance, is the encounter of the old with the new. Mary is now 'blessed... among women' (v. 42) and the one who probably recognises Elizabeth, an ageing Jewish woman, as the one from whom the last of the prophets of the old law is to be born. Mary's song (vv. 46–55) is radical—we could even call it a war song of liberation, a song of God's combat in human history; a testimony to God's plan to bring about a world of equal relationships, equal respect for every person, each one someone in whom God dwells. Interestingly, this image of a pregnant woman about to give birth to something extraordinary and new is itself an image of the work of God. Through the power of the Spirit, God brings about the new birth of men and women dedicated to justice and living out their relationship with God in loving relationships with each other. Mary's delivery of a son (2:7) arguably has a collective meaning involving every man and woman as it goes beyond the limits of human biology in signifying God's birth into humanity.

In Luke's two final references to Mary (vv. 34–35; 48–51) this collective significance is again attached to her. First, Simeon's prophecy seems to extend Mary's significance to all time and to all places. Those who struggle for God's kingdom will inevitably suffer hostility in this world and a sword will pierce the heart of the poor and those who strive for God's justice. Those who put God's concerns first and are filled with a passion for the liberation of their neighbours will be blessed. For me this shows Luke's concern to connect Mary firmly with the events of the cross and her sharing of Jesus' sufferings.

The second of these references brings us to those perplexing events surrounding Jesus at the age of twelve, talking to the scholars in the temple. Again, Mary clearly did not quite understand what was going on. Was this yet another memory lapse? Had she again forgotten the conversation she had had with the angel? As with the family tensions in Mark's Gospel, here is a further incident when Mary and the family were a little reluctant to come to terms fully with Jesus' vocation. This may well have been a well-known fact in those early days, and both Mark and Luke voice it in different ways and through different events.

It is also worth remembering that all that Luke shows about Jesus' childhood is retrospective (he was writing about 80 years after the events) and although the actual details may well be a little hazy, the theological value of what he is trying to emphasise is important. What Luke is saying is that, because this is the biggest thing that has ever happened in history, everything—values, traditions, customs, beliefs—is being completely turned upside down. For Luke, the events surrounding the birth of Jesus reverse every value system that has ever existed. Power, wealth and profit are no longer the strengths they once were, nor are they the measuring-stick that they had hitherto been. Throughout his Gospel, Luke is concerned with the last, the lost and the least. His agenda is specifically supportive of those on the edge and in this respect we should remember that it is only Luke who includes the parables of the good Samaritan, the prodigal son, the lost sheep and the lost coin.

Now, as a result of Mary's 'yes' and Jesus' birth and the vulnerability of it all, things cannot possibly ever be the same again. Towards the end of his life Jesus will again reveal the real strength of this vulnerability when the crown that many were expecting turned out to be a crown of thorns. This is at the very heart of Luke's mission—his concern with the vulnerable and the poor, the *anawim*—and it is so very clear in his unique portrayal of Mary.

The Acts of the Apostles, also believed to be the work of Luke, makes it clear that Mary was present at the 'birth' of the new Christian community as the gathered disciples met to persevere in prayer and remain united (Acts 1:14). Mary was there as mother, sister, friend, disciple and teacher of this new movement that had been organised by her son—a movement whose historical roots lie in the proclamation of the presence of the kingdom among the poor and those deprived of all recognition by the established powers.

John's deeply theological agenda

The Gospel of John presents Mary on two specific occasions, and on both occasions she is not mentioned by name. The first of these is the wedding at Cana (John 2:1–11) when Jesus, at her bidding, works the first of his miraculous signs, changing water into wine. Mary's faith in her son conceives and gives birth to the new community of God in the world, inaugurating a new time for God's people. This is the community of the kingdom, where poor and despised Cana of Galilee becomes the place where God's glory is revealed; indeed Cana itself is an *anawim* kind of place. It is interesting that in this episode Mary is only referred to in relation to her son, as the 'mother of Jesus'. For me the crucial part of the Cana episode is not that the assembled people were awestruck by a spectacular miracle but rather that the disciples came to believe in Jesus (v. 11). What we should note, though, is that Mary's belief in Jesus actually enabled the story to progress because it was only following her own moment of belief that she commanded the servants to get on with the mission: 'do whatever he tells you' (v. 5). Even before any miracle occurred, Mary believed in her son totally.

In this episode, just as in Mark and Luke, John preserves the tradition that there were tensions between Jesus and his mother. Unique to John, however, is the fact that the disciples, from the very outset of the Gospel, knew exactly who Jesus was and, possibly because of this, kept waiting for his miracles. But Jesus for the most part was reluctant to be open about his messianic identity, even with his mother.

All human family relationships—especially those between children and parents—have to be worked out gradually. Why should it have been so very different for Jesus and Mary?

All the so-called 'signs' in John's Gospel pointing to Jesus' true identity seem to disturb people enough for them to raise important questions but in order for 'glory' to be revealed, faith was needed. For those at Cana with eyes to see and hearts open to love, the revelation of God's glory was life-changing—transfiguring and liberating. Thus, once again, we come to the heart of what we mean by speaking of a life transfigured. God's glory is so often disclosed in very ordinary events such as a wedding in Cana. Suddenly, worlds can be changed and lives transformed by the grandeur of God, and people are invited to move on, transfigured and liberated. In Cana's simple marriage feast, a world was charged with glory and life took on a brand-new meaning as God himself rejoiced over the people as a bridegroom with a bride. Dare people believe that they can see the glory of God in the ordinary? That is the first step towards transfiguration.

The second of John's Mary episodes is at the foot of the cross (19:25–27) when Jesus is dying. Here Jesus entrusts his beloved disciple to his mother as her son and, in the line of great Old Testament maternal figures (Sarah, Hagar, Rachel, Hannah), Mary stands as the mother of the new community of men and women who have become followers of Jesus because they believe that God's glory was manifested in him. John's Gospel sets Mary at the centre of Jesus Christ's salvation event. She is the symbol of the people who welcome the message of the kingdom and the fullness of Word made flesh. There is also an ancient tradition that, following the resurrection of Jesus, John moved from Jerusalem to Ephesus and Mary accompanied him. Ephesus was the place where many early Christians believed she had died (the Dormition) and from where she was raised into heaven (the Assumption), and to this day pilgrims flock to Ephesus in order to visit 'Mary's House'. Interestingly, Ephesus was also the venue for the great Council that pronounced her 'mother of God' (*Theotokos*) in the year 431.

Again, Mary is not mentioned by her own name in John 19—she is simply 'woman'. By not even identifying her as his mother, Jesus is drawing attention away from his own blood relationship with Mary in order to focus attention on her as an individual whose faith has endured to the very end. The Gospel here is using typology—John is keen to show the way in which Mary is a 'type' of all whom Jesus loves and whose faith perseveres. Mary showed faith at Cana and at the cross, at the beginning and at the end of Jesus' earthly ministry.

But this is not simply an episode in which a son makes provision for his mother. Throughout his Gospel John infuses theological symbolism into the events he describes. I will return to the deep significance of this particular scene in Chapter 6 but for the moment I would like to focus on one aspect of it. Roman Catholic Christian traditions sometimes refer to Mary as the Mother of the Church. Although the term was not itself used in the life of the early Church, I think it could well find its roots here at the foot of the cross. Christians often imagine and debate when it was that the church per se was born—was it in Bethlehem's manger, was it around the table in the upper room, was it at Pentecost or could it have been at the foot of the cross? Jesus says to John, 'Behold thy mother' (v. 27, KJV). Now, if John is at the foot of the cross representing each one of us, then Mary does become the mother of the new community and quite possibly a birthday is celebrated even on Calvary.

Mary crowned in revelation

Finally, in Revelation 12 a woman appears clothed with the sun and crowned with stars. She is in labour and fighting a dragon. Her vocation is victory, to be the bride of the lamb, to be the New Jerusalem where all who keep God's commandments and bear witness to Jesus will finally be united. The persecuted and martyred people of God—the *anawim*—bear the pledge of Jesus' victory. Although the woman in Revelation 12 is probably an image of Israel as the mother of the Messianic saviour (Micah 4:9–10; Isaiah 66:7) and not a direct allusion to the physical birth of the Messiah in the incarnation, one could imagine that John may have had Mary in the back of his mind and thought that she related to that woman—the figure of the people's humble faith, the suffering people who believe in the crucified Saviour without losing hope. She is the figure of a church persecuted by the world, by the forces of the anti-kingdom and the powerful and the oppressors of every kind who, like the dragon in the book of Revelation, want to 'devour' the children and descendants of the woman. They seek even to devour the whole 'project' of the kingdom on earth, all that is life and liberation, all that is the mature fruit of the woman's fertile womb.

The new people of God, of whom Mary is the symbol and figure, is indeed the 'sign' that appears in heaven and on earth and that gave back to Eve's descendants the grace and the power to triumph over the serpent. From her flesh the Spirit formed God's incarnation. She symbolises the woman-people of God, from whose womb salvation has emerged, the sign of the community of those who keep God's commandments and bear witness to Jesus.

Part 2

Liberating signs of the kingdom of God

I have already mentioned that the liberation method is the approach that I am using in this book. Other possible models would include the empiricist approach—one that bases reflection on people's own experiences of God in particular and of the religious tradition generally. Such experiences are gathered, analysed and collated in various ways, producing a whole model of theologising based on the resulting data. There is also the pastoral approach, in which theological reflection is generally done as a response to particular pastoral situations or as part of the church's ministry in varying contexts.

The liberation approach starts from the premise that theology, as an activity performed by Christians, emerges from both the experience of living in the real world of human suffering and injustice, and the experience of being firmly rooted in the presence of God. It is keen to define the work of theology as an activity that does not shun suffering and injustice but rather encourages immersion in such crisis. Its basic hallmark is the challenge for Christians to meet issues of life head-on. By doing so, in our unjust world they stand in solidarity with all those who suffer injustice, and subsequently they embody all efforts to establish human freedom and dignity. So the liberation context is crucial—it encourages deep theological reflection and serious activity that touches every dimension of life. It is a reflective way completely 'in tune' with the biblical witness and it allows God's saving acts in history to penetrate every level of human existence.

The contemporary liberation approach to theology received its main impetus during the 1960s and was used to describe the response of various South American theologians to particular situations of oppression. Its proponents were greatly concerned with the role of the Church in such situations of injustice and placed a strong emphasis on the urgent need for social change, which distinguished them from mainstream church thinking. In 1968 there was a crucial meeting of the Roman Catholic Latin American Bishops' Conference at Medellín in Colombia at which significant dissatisfaction with the social and political state of affairs in South America was voiced.

The Medellín conference was followed a decade later by another one at Puebla, Mexico, and a further one at Santo Domingo in 1992.

The phrase 'preferential option for the poor' emerged formally from the Puebla conference in 1979 in the contributions of one of the leading liberation theologians of the 20th century, Gustavo Gutierrez. In using this phrase, Gutierrez recovered a much older Pauline principle, namely:

Consider your own call, brothers and sisters: not many of you were wise by human standards, not many were powerful, not many were of noble birth. But God chose what is foolish in the world to shame the wise; God chose what is weak in the world to shame the strong; God chose what is low and despised in the world, things that are not, to reduce to nothing things that are, so that no one might boast in the presence of God. He is the source of your life in Christ Jesus, who became for us wisdom from God, and righteousness and sanctification and redemption, in order that, as it is written, "Let the one who boasts, boast in the Lord."'

1 Corinthians 1:26–31

Connected to this rediscovery of Paul's call for liberation, the various conferences used terms such as 'inhuman misery' (Medellín, 1968), 'anti-evangelical poverty' (Puebla, 1979) and 'intolerable extremes of misery' (Santo Domingo, 1992) to describe the plight of thousands of people in Latin American countries. Medellín summarised such a plight as 'institutionalised violence', which in turn violated God's intention to build the kingdom. This divine intention offered life in all its abundance and it was the lack of such abundance that led liberation theologians to claim that God sided primarily with the poor and those at risk.

As the liberationist approach became more widespread, a substantial number of priests began to join revolutionary groups, not only growing more revolutionary in their theology but also aligning themselves with actual military forces. Powerful statements such as 'bias to the poor' were used and the revolutionary priests and theologians encouraged the Catholic Church in South America to adopt this way of responding theologically to the needs of the people. Such a theology insisted that theologians should be committed to action as well as reflection and prayer—and this implied a commitment to taking sides with those who were struggling to free the oppressed, even if this led to participation in political revolution, and even if it led to violence. Liberating God's children had to mean going beyond the traditional terms of 'salvation' and 'redemption'.

In an article in *The Guardian* (14 December 2012) on how the poor people of Brazil desperately need the Church today to revive its role as a force for political change, Giles Fraser reminds us that the Vatican was very opposed to the idea of liberation theology. In the 1970s Rome was angry that an increasing number of Catholic priests were behaving as revolutionaries. Gradually the Vatican took steps to end church involvement with the liberation movement by appointing a succession of conservative bishops. The Roman Catholic Church believed that liberation theology was too dangerously close to Marxism—an ideology loathed by Pope John Paul II, originally from Poland. As Prefect of the 'Congregation for the Doctrine of the Faith', Cardinal Ratzinger (later Pope Benedict XVI) took a firm line in opposing any moves towards sympathising with the Liberation theologians. However, with the accession of Pope Francis I, there has been a noticeable softening of attitude.

Christ at the centre of all things

The 1968 Medellín Conference insisted, however, that it was the New Testament that lay at the heart of the liberation rationale and not some other political and secular philosophy. Essentially the conference emphasised four significant things. First, that both the figure and experience of Christ must be approached directly from a concern with God's saving acts. Second, that both the divinity and humanity of Christ are balanced so that the poor as a people, and poverty as a scandal, are placed at the heart of the person of Christ. Third, that the presence of Christ be understood essentially in terms of current situations rather than as a figure of history. Christians were encouraged to participate fully and without reserve in the longing for total redemption and the transformation of society. Fourth, that the presence of Christ is quintessentially seen in the poor and the oppressed. This is not necessarily where human beings would like to meet him, but it is where he actually is, however uncomfortable this context might be for some people.

The appeal of this liberation approach is that it offers an effective way both to engage theologically with the world and to reflect on the ways in which the spiritual life impinges on daily living. It effectively serves as a programme to help Christians realise that living a life of faith in the world today, with open eyes and an open heart for the real problems of people, is an enormous and unavoidable challenge. It challenges Christians to break out of an individualist and elitist mould and to begin listening to the Bible in fresh ways.

Engaging with the biblical witness

How do we evaluate the biblical witness to this way of engaging with theology? Or to put it another way—what grounding in the New Testament can really be claimed for liberation theology? Interestingly, in many ways it is not difficult to justify it on the basis of the Old Testament, many of whose writers see God operating in the sphere of national and international politics. Indeed, they regard this political sphere as the very place where God's people are called to respond directly to his presence and activity. But how does the New Testament resonate with it?

Critics of the liberation approach usually argue that the New Testament does not offer a coherent rallying call to transform the structures of society. Rather, they detect a withdrawal from concern with the public world of politics. They question whether belief in the incarnation and in the redemptive effects of Christ's death and resurrection relate in any way to the radical claims made by the proponents of liberation theology. Arguably, in the time of the Gospels and the early Church there was a general assumption that world history was very shortly to come to an end. There was a feeling that a decisive divine event would happen quite soon and that the kingdom of God would be fully inaugurated. This would give a very good reason why Jesus' non-political attitude cannot be regarded as normative for the Church today. Who knows but that the intensity of his own expectation of the kingdom may have produced in his mind a radical contraction of the time span which must elapse before its final manifestation? The fact that history continued was itself a display that the time of the end was not yet. And so, like the people of God in the Old Testament, the early Christians became increasingly concerned with seeking new ways of working out the divine purpose within an ongoing history of the world.

In the New Testament itself we see the beginnings of the re-adjustment to the delay of the end. After Luke had written his Gospel, he began to write the history of the Church (Acts), setting it within the framework of secular history. That is at least a hint that continuing history has some significance for the divine plan of salvation. Further evidence can be found in the fact that the New Testament writers give the risen Christ the divine title, *Kyrios* (Lord). We see them beginning to transfer to Christ some of the functions that in the Old Testament belong to God as Lord—the prophetic day of the Lord (see, for example, Isaiah 13 or Joel 1:15) becomes the day of the Lord Jesus Christ (2 Corinthians 1:14; 1 Corinthians 5:5; 2 Thessalonians 2:2; 2 Peter 3:10. In Isaiah the title 'Lord' is ascribed to the God who is seen as the sovereign ruler of world history, the God who makes use of the imperial power of Cyrus of Persia to rescue the Jews from their exile in Babylon (Isaiah 45). Transference of the title to Christ would suggest that Christ also exercises sovereignty over the nations and their history. If this is so, it follows that the political and social movements of which history is made up cannot possibly be a matter of indifference to Christians.

The New Testament also claims that Christ fulfils all the promises of God recorded in scripture (2 Corinthians 1:20) and the author of the Acts of the Apostles recognises some of the messianic promises as fulfilled by the risen Christ working through his Church. When Paul is describing his conversion to Agrippa, he is represented as saying that the Lord was sending him to the Gentiles 'to open their eyes, that they may turn from darkness to light' (Acts 26:18). Interestingly, the opening of 'the eyes of the blind' is a prominent theme in the prophecies of Isaiah (Isaiah 42:7), so Luke may well be seeing Paul as also fulfilling Old Testament prophecy through his activity as an apostle.

Continuing history is then the period of time within which the promises of the Old Testament are further brought to fulfilment, and may be brought to this fulfilment by Christ working through his Church. Some of these promises are very much concerned with political and social justice, with the liberation of the oppressed, and with the establishment of peace between nations (Micah 4:1–4; Isaiah 11; 42:1–7). It may be that one aspect of the purpose of continuing history is that these social and political promises should eventually obtain some kind of provisional fulfilment in social and political terms. Perhaps also, this fulfilment should be achieved through the involvement of the Church in movements for political and social justice. If this is so, then Christians today should find themselves driven back to the Old Testament to find the meaning for their collective existence in their various national and political groupings, as well as for guidance as to the principles which should inform godly political action.

However, the Christian is still called to read the Old Testament in the light of the New. Clearly, the Church must learn from the Old Testament about social justice and about the liberating powers of God, and certainly Christians must engage in political action. But effective political action derives from the possession of effective political power, and the Christ whom Paul sees as the manifestation of the power of God is actually the crucified Christ, the Christ who is wholly deprived of power as this world understands it. So one of the hardest tasks the Church has to face, on both the intellectual and the practical level, is to discover how these two possibly contradictory forms of power can be brought together.

Mary—woman of contradiction

What I want to convey in the next two chapters is that, in the witness of Mary, it is in fact possible to bring together these two forms of power. Firmly rooting our quest for Mary in the context of liberation enables us to begin seeing how her life was essentially a witness to the liberating powers of God. But this involves not only Mary's own liberation but ours, too, and from liberation comes the possibility of a more splendid transfigured life. Placing Mary in a liberation context is not in any way about 'modernising her' or making her the champion of emancipation on the basis, for instance, of her song of liberation at the beginning of Luke's Gospel (1:46–55). To do that would be to do both Mary and the wider ethos of the New Testament a serious injustice. The quest cannot simply be about bringing Mary as she stands in the gospels 'up to date', inadequately fitting her into modern patterns and modern values. Rather, it is about recognising her as a contradiction to modern patterns, values and ways of doing things. The Anglican theologian John Macquarrie picks this up in his book *Mary for all Christians* (T & T Clark, 2001) and states that she contradicts three things in particular: the neglect of the personal, the assertiveness of modern structures, and the individualism of modern men and women. He encourages his readers to hold these together in their 'provisional contradictoriness' so that each may correct and enrich the other. What is interesting is that this approach helps us to recognise why devotions to Mary do and should vary from age to age—it is precisely because the tensions between her affirmative qualities and her challenges to the contemporary age vary from one generation to another.

What will be my guiding principle as I consider Mary in these ways? It is the idea of the kingdom of God, which becomes of paramount significance as Christians seek ways to combine the witness of Mary in the Gospels and liberation-orientated theological engagement today. I want to read Mary's story in terms of the different images that the kingdom of God assumes in scripture, tradition and human experience. Her story is a story that makes present the signs of God's kingdom, the particular actions that reveal the presence of salvation in human history. Mary's story speaks of God and the kingdom, of divinity in a simple woman's life. It also speaks of the Son of God, who is born of a woman, and of the many children engendered by the Spirit of God who are born not of the flesh but of God (see John 1:12–13). To view Mary from the kingdom perspective enables us to see her passion for the poor, her passion for God's justice. By doing it in this way we are better able to recover through her story the force of the Spirit acting on people, and especially women, in every age. In one sense, her story is one that calls for the recovery of a 'subversive memory'—a dangerous memory. This is a memory capable of changing situations because it not only keeps alive the hopes and struggles of people in the past but gives life and growth to a universal solidarity among people—and again, especially among women—past, present and future.

With this guiding principle in mind I feel it is no longer possible for us to view Mary simply as a mother who is subject to a son, even a son who is also the Son of God. To do this is to continue to define women as subjects—subject to men, whether they be fathers, husbands, sons or some other controlling male in a woman's personal or professional life. This is what I meant when I said earlier that Mary is more than simply a humble, lowly and obedient woman. Of course she is the mother of 'gentle' Jesus but she is a working mother concerned primarily with harvesting the kingdom—she is an active member of the movement of the poor, just as her son was.

Chapter 3

Divinely chosen, kingdom worker

The opening of John's Gospel brings us to the heart of our Christian faith. Here John seeks to lay before his readers three absolutes: the pre-existence of Christ and his activity in the whole process of creation; Christ's activity in guiding and illuminating humanity; that the incarnation of Christ enables human beings to reclaim their rightful place in the story of God's creation and redemption. All three of these absolutes are integral to the process of human liberation.

Whatever the controversies surrounding the various traditions associated with Mary—practices, prayers, images, beliefs—one thing is certain: she has a special role to play in the story of God's liberating creation and redemption. Mary's motherhood is the linchpin of the doctrine of the incarnation. The early Church recognised this from the beginning, when it had to defend first the humanity and then the divinity of Christ against a variety of heretical thinking. I find it arrogant when people accuse Christians of being the recipients of superstitious mumbo-jumbo from an ignorant, bygone age. Those first Christians were not only preaching a message that had a particular appeal for those who lived on the margins of the Roman empire—women, slaves, the poor and so on. They were also equipping minds to make sense of how the story of Christ fulfilled and challenged philosophical claims about the relationship between matter and spirit, humanity and divinity.

Mary's motherhood—and more than simply motherhood—made her the first person of the new creation in Christ. As a symbol, she allows us to contemplate what we are all invited to become in a world without violence (in every sense of that word) and where love triumphs. In this sense, we could argue that we will not fully understand Jesus without first coming to terms with his mother—basically, if we mess up Mary, we run the risk of messing up Jesus! The two are intimately linked.

In several parts of the world—mainly in predominantly Roman Catholic areas—it is interesting that so many people seem to connect to Jesus as their Saviour and hope, particularly those living in the midst of violence and injustice, through first creating an intimate and personal love for his mother. In much the same way, Christians in the medieval period showed a particular devotion to the humanity and suffering of Jesus through a love of Mary—admittedly the devotion was a little excessive at times! Clearly, I think, there is a strong case to be made that a deep respect and love for Mary does in fact provide a strong defence against the dangers of concentrating too much devotion on the humanity of Jesus to the detriment of his divinity. The overall reason for any devotion to Mary is that Jesus is divine and Marian devotion is a firm safeguard for this divinity.

For me, any exploration of Mary must be made from a Christological perspective and her motherhood is first and foremost linked to the divinity of Christ. This is why I think that many people opt to pursue the particularity of the role Mary plays in the quest for liberation, especially in those parts of the world struggling for justice. I am constantly astounded at the way so many people in those contexts turn to Mary and her story, as they grapple with life's perplexities and injustices. For so many of them, Mary has a distinctive role to play as they seek to discover a Christ-centred counter-cultural way of living and approaching their conundrums—after all isn't this what lies at the heart of the Christian faith (Matthew 5–7)? In Chapter 4 I will go on to unpack some of the theological questions surrounding Mary's virginity and motherhood in the light of liberation and the way in which these can be rooted in the grace of a transfigured life.

Kingdom worker

It was the writings of two women from South America that originally inspired me to begin the journey of locating Mary within both a kingdom and liberation context. Through their writings I have begun to understand more fully some of the implications of Mary's life for people today. Ivone Gebara, a religious sister in São Paulo, and Maria Clara Bingemar, an academic and a mother working in Rio de Janeiro, in their *Mary: Mother of God, Mother of the Poor* (Burns and Oates, 1989), have influenced much of my thinking concerning Mary both as having a continuing liberationist ministry on the one hand, and, on the other, as having been liberated herself.

The main reason why I think it is essential to interpret Mary from deep within a Christological perspective is precisely because the kingdom of God is what provides the context for her whole life and ministry—this is the only basis from which to approach Mary in liberationist theology. The experience of the kingdom of God gathers together so much theology, providing focus for uniting God's saving activity in history and the subsequent ministry of Christians throughout the generations who have continued God's mission on earth. Constantly in his ministry Jesus was confronted by both his disciples and his detractors as to the precise nature of the kingdom that he proclaimed. People were keen to know how they could enter it and inherit it (Luke 10:25; 18:18). Consistently, his response was that to enter it meant embracing and accepting the poor, the destitute, those excluded by purity laws and those discarded and left to exist on the margins of society, as opposed to living the abundant life he so earnestly sought to share with his followers. At every given opportunity, Jesus insisted that to do this was to share fully in the work (and mission) of God and to further the inauguration of God's kingdom more fully on earth. So experience of the kingdom of God must lie at the heart of Mary's story and our interpretation and understanding of that story. It is this that provides the correct basis for recognising all that Mary was—both in the New Testament and subsequently in the developing Christian tradition and experience.

Gebara and Bingemar argue that Jesus' proclamation of the kingdom—both in word and in action—was in fact a hugely multifaceted and diverse experience that touched every part of the fabric of human existence. Jesus' picture of the kingdom showed that it could be encountered through amazingly unexpected channels. One could discover it in precious pearls (Matthew 13:45–46), lost coins (Luke 15:8–10), the birds of the air (Matthew 6:26), sharing bread (14:13–21), the pouring of perfume (John12:1–8), washing one another's feet (13:1–11). Jesus was able to identify marks of the kingdom even in mustard seeds (Luke 13:18–19), in the poverty of widows (Mark12:41–44), in the ways in which humans can be healed (Luke 4:38–39), in taking time to stop and chat besides wells (John 4:5–26), in watching women mixing yeast (Matthew 13:33) and in showing affection to children (19:13–15).

The ordinary becomes the extraordinary

For Jesus, the kingdom was something that could be spotted very easily—it is part and parcel of life as it is lived by ordinary men and women in every age. In a theological context these ordinary aspects of human living easily slip into the realm of the extraordinary—they all become channels through which it is possible to seek the energy to live God's life on earth. So the kingdom of God is constantly the extraordinary being rooted firmly in the ordinariness of life. Ordinary life can become a channel through which the divine spark can be recognised and shared. By sharing this, something that can have a profound impact is stirred up in human hearts—this is the 'stuff' that can undo selfishness and injustice and, by turning towards the needs of the poor and needy, human beings begin walking in the direction of God's kingdom.

It is in this sense that many Catholic Christians, particularly in the developing world, regard Mary with a special spiritual poignancy. For so many of them, Mary speaks of a God who has revealed himself fully to a vulnerable young woman and she, in turn, speaks to them of a distinctive spirituality that can be experienced by women facing injustice in deeply entrenched patriarchal societies. She speaks to them about the Son of God who was born of a woman and about a special relationship between a woman, a child, Spirit and even God. There is no doubt that any exploration of Mary in a liberation theology must come to terms with the issues surrounding her femininity.

I find the approach that Gebara and Bingemar take particularly inspiring. By affirming positively that God's salvation and creation are inseparably present in both women and men—not one without the other—they open up a new and radical way of understanding the significance of the femininity of Mary. This way of working with the fact of Mary's femininity radically changes the insistence on having a traditional hierarchy of patriarchal values—one that has unquestionably left a deep and possibly damaging imprint both on theology and the life of women in the church. When a patriarchal culture becomes the starting point, the inevitable consequence is that women immediately become subordinate and sometimes even nameless in history. Reflecting theologically in a kingdom context refuses to bow to such starting points. Instead, it leads to a much greater respect for both the complexity and complementarity of the two significant elements that make up the reality of human nature—male and female. It is a strong and definite affirmation that God's salvation and creation activity has always and inseparably unfolded itself and shown itself to be present fully in both sexes.

Approaching Mary in this way does not mean that liberation theologians present a completely new scenario offering the very opposite of a patriarchal culture. It is not a matter of switching from a patriarchal to a matriarchal framework and hoping that all will be well. Rather, it means seeking to reveal something of the full reality of human nature in all its multiplicity, diversity and richness. Seeing Mary's life and role unfold from within a liberation context is about recognising that, if she is not included fully in God's saving action in Christ, something integral gets left out. Without the female dimension that she symbolises, half of human identity is lost—and consequently half of the divine is presumably also lost as God made all of us in his own image (Genesis 1:27).

This liberation vision, as an authentic entry point into an

exploration of Mary's story, is a strong affirming statement that she cannot simply be seen as the enchanting mother of a gentle Jesus. Mary is, above all else, a strong kingdom worker and an advocate for the poor and those suffering injustice. Liberation theology severs Mary from mere submissiveness to her son—an attitude that has been a damaging expression of the submission of women to the established order of a prevailing patriarchal system. The struggles of people all over the world recognise in Mary lasting and hopeful signs of a powerful new light shining from Nazareth. Hope for the kingdom of God is hope for authentic human completeness and fulfilment. It is a deep yearning for the unlimited horizons of the kingdom to be actualised. It is seeing the extraordinary in the midst of the ordinary. Allowing Mary's story to become an intrinsic part of the kingdom story is to move closer to discovering the complete man, the complete woman, the complete world, the complete God. These become the man, the woman, the world and the God of all poor people's most heartfelt yearning—indeed, the yearning of the *anawim* that occurs throughout the biblical narrative.

Liberation is the work of God

There is a danger that all of this can sometimes appear to be an attempt to contrive something theological that is not necessarily there—having the feel of artifice and exaggeration about it. What balances it all out for me is the fact that, throughout the Bible, God always manifests himself as functioning primarily for the liberation of the oppressed and the poor. Because the Israelites were often a rejected and ridiculed people, it was their experience and perception of actually being God's chosen people that rooted their efforts to sustain their dignity and their determination to discover liberation.

One of the aspects of Marian devotion throughout the world that has interested me is the existence of real physical places at which Mary is supposed to have revealed herself to individuals. In consequence those places have become extremely popular sites of spiritual and religious pilgrimage—Glastonbury and Walsingham in England, Medjugorje in Bosnia, Lourdes and La Salette in France, Knock in Ireland, Częstochowa in Poland, Fatima in Portugal, Montserrat in Spain, as well as many others. What is interesting is that the 'encounter' that happens between particular individuals and Mary in these places has had a similar effect to seeking a universal dignity and fairness in society. Such encounters have provided lasting and significant impetus for discipleship among diverse Christian peoples—usually very ordinary people (*anawim*) and not bishops and princesses!

Mary of Guadalupe

Perhaps one of the most famous of these is the appearance of Mary to a poor Indian named Juan Diego at Tepeyac, on the periphery of present-day Mexico City, in 1531. Although initially a local event, what has become known today as 'Our Lady of Guadalupe' has grown from being the 'Lady of the Indians', to being the first Lady of Mexico, to being declared the Patroness of Latin America by Pope John Paul II. Today Mary of Guadalupe is rapidly being recognised by more and more people from Canada to Argentina as the Mother of the Americas, north and south. I focus on this particular appearance of Mary because, firstly, it is located in a place of significance for liberation theology, and secondly, it is widely accepted that the subsequent devotion offered to Mary in Guadalupe is, in fact, indicative of an ongoing and significant development of a much wider Christian understanding of God himself, as opposed to such devotion being exclusively Marian.

It is a sad and well-known fact that violence, rape and death marked the birth of Latin America and that the Christian European invasion, beginning at the end of the 15th century, initiated a process of extermination, enslavement and exploitation. However, in the midst of this horror, the Guadalupe story relates that Juan Diego climbed to the top of Tepeyac Hill—the site of an ancient sanctuary signifying the feminine aspects of the native god Tonantzin—and had a revelation of Mary. She, in turn, declared to him: 'Know and understand that I am Mary, the ever-virgin and mother of the Lord, through whom we live; he is the creator, the Lord of all that is near and of our togetherness, he is the Lord of heaven and earth.' What is striking about the original accounts of this particular revelation is that, at its roots, it actually sought unity between the Spanish and the native Indian traditions—a mixture of languages and images was used. As a result, there would no longer be the radical opposition between two traditions that had dominated the affairs of Guadalupe for too long. After many unsuccessful attempts on the part of the missionaries to conquer the natives, a new path for mutually enriching religious dialogue was opened through what they saw as Mary's continuing ministry. There was a reversal of roles—originally, the Spanish were the missionaries to the Indians, but through the Guadalupe revelation, the Indians became missionaries to the Spanish. The Indians were no longer simply the passive recipients of a foreign culture, but rather, they became active agents in the construction of a new understanding of faith. It was no longer a question of masters and subjects—them and us—but one of equal partners in a common search for the true God.

Guadalupe functioned in much the same way as some of the liberation accounts in the Old Testament. Over the years, however, many people have sought ways to manipulate Guadalupe so as to take away the fullness of its liberating impact—such as seeing it as a 'nice place' to visit. Nevertheless, that impact has not been lost and millions of Roman Catholic Christians continue to flock to that place. They see in it an evangelising process that is of its very nature ecumenical because it brings about dialogue at the level of different people's image of God. Guadalupe continues to initiate this dialogue and the result has been the beginning of a new religious unity that neither alienates the zealous missionaries of Western Christianity nor deprives the natives of Mexico of their deep spiritual heritage. At the roots of Mexican Christianity lie new life and unity, not through eradication and oppression, but through synthesis and sharing. From a desperate situation of perplexity and fear, Guadalupe moved people to a sense of godly amazement.

Today, through the writings of various theologians from different traditions, Mexican Christianity continues to open up exciting new ways of understanding God and his working in the world, but entering into this new adventure means journeying through the voices and struggles of the oppressed throughout the world. God is always faithful when his ways are recognised and acted upon, and his faithfulness leads us to the fullness of truth through heeding the cries of the little ones of the world—the *anawim* (Luke 10:21). There is, however, a real sense in which 'doing' theology through the lenses of Western perspectives can erect barriers that prevent us from fully understanding the true creativity of Guadalupe and other places like it. In the main, such Western perspectives tend to focus, sometimes exclusively, on the metaphor of God's paternity, to the detriment of the maternal-feminine face of God, which also appears in the biblical narrative (Matthew 23:37; Luke 13:34). Of course, this has historical influences—in the masculine-dominated feudal world of the Middle Ages a strong devotion to Mary had a certain impact on Catholic popular devotion that tended to focus on her alone. The question is whether this devotion ever led to a new way of thinking about God which would have revitalised understanding of the biblical feminine aspects of the God of history.

The feminine heritage of Guadalupe

Originally, the Guadalupe experience led to liberation from religious oppression and, as such, meant that an image of an exclusively male God could no longer be comprehended. In the native Indian psyche everything that is perfect and whole has both a male and a female component—the cosmos, creation, human personality and even God. These two integral aspects are not contradictory but complementary and as the paternal-male aspect of God is the all-powerful creator and giver of life, the maternal-feminine aspect, typified by Guadalupe, is the all-powerful suppliant. An understanding of the feminine aspect was added to the God of the Christians, and the personal dimension was added to traditional Indian religious belief, leading to a profound enrichment of both. The American theologian Virgil Elizondo, who works mainly in poor US American neighbourhoods, sees in the Guadalupe revelation a redemptive and expanding mutuality of two religious traditions, resulting in a new, specifically Mexican expression of Christianity ('Mary and the Poor' in *Mary in the Churches,* edited by Hans Küng and Jürgen Moltmann, Concilium168, T & T Clark, 1983). In reality, at the heart of all this is a faith commitment that proclaims unashamedly that the supreme gift of this maternal-feminine and paternal-male image is Jesus of Nazareth, who came to give his life for the sake of the whole of creation—offering a very different way of encountering God. Guadalupe consistently refers to Jesus as the Saviour and, using native Indian symbols, recognises Jesus as the centre of the universe. Through the revelation of Mary to these people, the Lord becomes incarnated deeply into their cultural soil and, out of this particular incarnation of the gospel, a new church is constantly being reborn—one that values and is rooted in its ever-changing local context

What I find striking about Guadalupe is the role it played in restoring to an exploited people a religious identity that also helped them to build a new national identity. This has deep implications that go far beyond Mexico. It helps our more general understanding of any conquered people who stand up with confidence, refusing to allow their culture to die, seeking new ways to ensure its continuity and enabling it to serve them as both a source and summit of a transfigured life, strengthening them to own and become who they truly are.

A liberating Mary

We have focused in this chapter mainly on issues surrounding the femininity of Mary and some of the challenges that face us when we explore that fully. In many ways we could expect that Mary's story would have greater significance for women in general. Ironically, this is not always the case—ambiguity as to her real significance for women continues to prevail. Indeed, Mary and her story are often rejected even by some feminist theologians as lacking any possible useful symbolism. This deficit is probably for a number of reasons, primarily for the fact that much of her image is the creation of a predominantly male church. Her image also seems to place social and religious constraints on women, having been created by male theologians who so often fail to listen to and hear the true voices of women. It is also a view of Mary that sometimes forms an obstacle to ecumenism as well as being one that creates ambivalence with regard to the Church's attitudes to human sexuality.

There is a danger, of course, that when we begin to play with images, they become closed because those who like such images exactly as they are resist any change, refusing to allow them to open up to new references and comparisons. Images can also be idolised, too often becoming absolute and stereotypical. For far too long women have been caught up in all of this—especially in the Church! In so many different ways, Mary has been reduced to a level of rigid principle that makes it difficult for her to be a source of fresh and vital inspiration to help make women crucial figures of the faith—especially in the West.

Another feminist theologian who has influenced my thinking about Mary is the late Dutch theologian Catharina Halkes, who specialised in feminism and Christianity. She draws attention to the occasion when Mary visits her cousin Elizabeth (Luke 1:39–45), pointing out that Mary does not become enraptured because she is pregnant. Rather, she glorifies God's liberating action precisely because she is herself the liberated Israel—those of low degree who are exalted (*anawim*) ('Mary and Women' in *Mary in the Churches*, edited by Hans Küng and Jürgen Moltmann, Concilium 168, T & T Clark, 1983). Significantly, her song of triumph (vv. 46–55) occurs in the context of a meeting between two women, both of whom are playing a significant role in the history of God's salvation. Gebara and Bingemer express this well when they state that both women were pregnant with the prophetic life itself, and that it was the spark of the Spirit that leapt across between them, raising Elizabeth up above herself and causing the child to move in her womb. It is this that provides Mary with her prophetic vision.

For Catharina Halkes the song is, as it were, a radical and subversive prelude to the Sermon on the Plain and the address of Jesus in Luke 6. In other words, Jesus' message is first and foremost intended for all those marginalised people who are summed up in this 'insignificant' woman. Because of her faithfulness and her belief in the Messiah, Mary is a good personification of the Church as the messianic Israel. But this is only so when the image is viewed, quite radically and with its most profound consequences, as pointing to a self-emptying and loss of power which is accompanied by an utter transfiguration of self into the service of others. God emptied himself and became pure service in Christ, and Christ emptied himself to liberate fully his people. In much the same way, Mary's task was to continue God's liberating activity in the world. The last shall be first, and those who rule must, on their way to the kingdom, join the ranks of the poor, whose example is Mary.

The balance between male and female

Mary, then, in the context of feminist theological thinking is, for me as a male writer, a minefield—but certainly one that is worth exploring carefully! In this minefield I have become far less concerned with whether Mary is an appropriate role model for women or not or whether she is simply a token woman at the heart of what some see as a fundamentally patriarchal, anti-feminist religion; I am much more concerned with how she opens up ways which empower all of us to discover an authentic liberating balance between masculinity and femininity within ourselves. In an interesting essay, 'Feminist theology: a view of Mary' (in William McLoughlin and Jill Pinnock, editors, *Mary is for Everyone*, Gracewing, 1997), the Anglican theologian Ann Loades makes a key point regarding this kind of balancing act. She says that, as well as at one level honouring women and teaching them new aspirations, the Christian tradition has undercut that honour and aspiration by teaching women a disabling gender construction, and this is why it has by no means fostered a whole personhood in women.

This must surely be the crucial reason for rooting Mary in liberation theology—an authentic, balanced and respected wholeness emerges out of the process of liberating both the divine and the human in order to bring together femininity and masculinity. Ann Loades goes on to say that 'gender' refers primarily to what a particular society makes of relationships between males and females, and no society lives free of gender constructs. What we can do at the least is attend to these gender constructs and evaluate them—especially when they are conveyed by religious symbols—as realities which may help us to lay hold of, or be laid hold of by, the spiritual realities beyond what we see or think about. The object is not to obliterate differences, but to value them appropriately, and this need not mean that all those associated with men and masculinity are put at the top of some hierarchy of value, with those associated with women and femininity put at the bottom.

Human beings need to give and to receive from one another in as open and reciprocal way as they can. What is truly, and, I believe, urgently, needed is a renewed vision of wholeness—what it means to be male and female together—and a renewed vision of co-inherence between men and women. In this way each—male and female—can actualise the dignity and worth of the other, and the symbol of Mary surely lies at the heart of this.

Ann Loades draws attention to an important point made by another Anglican theologian, Elaine Storkey, in her article 'The significance of Mary for feminist theology' (in D. Wright, editor, *Chosen by God,* Marshall Pickering, 1989). Elaine Storkey continues the theme of gender balance and says that by giving birth to the Saviour, Mary was not in the least demeaned. It was not a symbol of the arrogance of male patriarchy but rather 'a statement of the humility of a non-gendered God who was prepared to come in human, sexual form'. As a male writer commenting on some key feminist theological reflection, I am greatly encouraged by Loades and Storkey. Both these theologians have taught me that the real thrust of feminist theology is about a humanly inclusive theology that carries with it the hope and the necessity that Christians can envision the mystery of God in gender-inclusive ways. Surely the reality is that the female and the feminine can of and by itself represent God, as is the case with the male. As Ann Loades rightly says, I think, both genders are as capable or incapable of imaging the mystery of God, and Mary is a highly appropriate 'symbol' through which to point us accurately towards grasping something of that mystery.

One final challenge

Some would argue that there is a sense in which the earth itself is female as mother earth. Interestingly, some also believe that this mother earth goes through a kind of menstrual cycle and that at key moments in that cycle, the moon—itself seen as a feminine entity—is renewed. In this cycle even the tides of the seas are affected, as if the latter was the very blood of the earth out of which all life emerges and through which all life is continually nourished and sustained. The twelfth-century spiritual writer Hildegard of Bingen said, 'The earth is at the same time Mother. She is Mother of all, for contained in her are the seeds of all. The earth of humankind contains all moistness, all verdancy, all germinating power. It is in so many ways fruitful. Yet it forms not only the basic raw material for humankind but also the substance of God's Son' ('A Call to Prayer', used for Earth Day 1990, *Interfaith Declarations and Worship Resources,* North American Conference on Religion and Ecology).

I recently listened to a fascinating, if not extremely challenging, spoken presentation by the musician Antony Hegerty ('Future Feminism' on the album *Cut the World* by Antony and the Johnsons, 2013) in which he called for the urgent feminisation of the deity. He claimed that contemporary humanity is at a critical threshold and hope lies deep within the femininity of life—all levels of life—and that the major religious institutions are in a highly significant place to lead the masses to understand this. Hegerty believes that this could potentially offer people a great deal of hope. Admittedly, for a good many, this could sound very far-fetched! However, in the context of reflecting theologically on life by way of liberation, and alongside all that has been said about Mary, I don't believe it to be quite as far-fetched as some would claim. I certainly believe that there is a ring of kingdom urgency about it.

Chapter 4

Virgin mother, profoundly human

In the light of what I have said in the previous chapter about Mary as liberator and kingdom worker, how do we go about interpreting and understanding possibly the profoundest of all the claims made about Mary—her very intimate relationship with God and her virginity?

By the power of the Holy Spirit

The Nicene Creed states: 'He came down from heaven; by the power of the Holy Spirit he became incarnate from the Virgin Mary, and was made man.' Essentially, the Nicene Fathers, in their reflections on the divine origin of Christ and the virgin birth, remained faithful to the Gospels of Matthew and Luke. Both evangelists are clear that the Messiah Jesus of Nazareth was 'begotten' by the Holy Spirit in the woman Mary. They are in agreement that the mother of Jesus was pregnant, not through having had sexual intercourse with a man, but by the working of the Holy Spirit. For both Matthew and Luke, the action of the Holy Spirit in the womb of Mary is the foundation for Christ's divine sonship (Luke 1:35; Matthew 1:18). Working quite independently of each other, both evangelists seem to be saying that Jesus is the Son of God by shifting the divine sonship of Jesus back from the Easter experience into the time before his birth or even into God's eternity.

In his book *The Birth of the Messiah* (G. Chapman, 1977) the Roman Catholic biblical scholar Raymond Brown makes an interesting point regarding the link between the pre-existence of Jesus and the virgin birth. To talk in terms of the virgin birth is to claim that God's creative action 'begets' Jesus to some degree in his conception in the womb as Son of God. On the other hand, to talk in terms of Jesus' pre-existence is, in reality, to be less concerned about the actual way Jesus was conceived. In this sense, the conception of Jesus is simply the beginning of the earthly career of the heavenly Son. Brown notes that it is no accident that John never speaks of the 'begetting' of Jesus, for Jesus simply *is* ('I am'—see John 8:58). With the development of Christian theology both these aspects were harmonised, so that the pre-existent Jesus was described as taking flesh (John 1:14) in the womb of the virgin Mary (Matthew 1:18; Luke 1:35). The virginal conception was no longer seen merely as a 'begetting' of God's Son but as the incarnation of the pre-existent Son of God, and that became orthodox Christian doctrine.

Matthew's agenda

By the time that Matthew was composing his Gospel, ties with the Jewish tradition had to all intents and purposes been broken; Jerusalem had been lost and with it the Christian community in the holy city. At about the same time there may well have been a deep sense of disappointment among the followers of Jesus that the kingdom of God had not been fully inaugurated and so they had to assert themselves again in the face of continuing persecution. Matthew's main contribution to this new sense of assertion was to collect and collate existing theological traditions to write his Gospel account. His agenda, as I see it, was attempting to formulate a new Christian synthesis out of traditional materials. This synthesis would provide his church with an adequate explanation of its origin and nature, as it tried to bridge the gap between a predominantly Jewish past and an increasingly Gentile future.

Matthew's Jesus appears as the fulfiller of Old Testament promises, as the son of David and as the new Moses. With Matthew, the title 'Son of God' has central prominence. There is no trace here of Mark's 'messianic secret'—it's all upfront! There does appear to be something of a paradox as this Son of God, born of a virgin, is ultimately shown to be God's revelation in the lowly form of the humiliated and crucified Jesus. However, before all of that, Matthew painstakingly presents his Jesus as being endowed with a unique divine authority—witness the miraculous actions (Matthew 8:23–27), the striking proclamations (chapters 5—7) and, of course, the virgin birth.

In essence, then, Matthew's presentation of Jesus seeks to show that it is actually the 'kingdom of God' that is released from a kind of heavenly concealment and made public through the miraculous birth of Jesus; through Mary a kingdom is ushered in from pre-existence to real existence. No longer is Mary simply a worker in and for the kingdom; she is actually the bearer of it.

Luke's agenda

Much the same can be said about Luke's agenda but this time with Gentile-Christian concerns. By basing the divine sonship of Jesus on the action of the Holy Spirit (Luke 1:35), Luke is making a strong case against any suggestion that Jesus was 'adopted' as the Son of God at some later stage in his earthly ministry. Luke is keen to stress that Jesus, through the power of the Holy Spirit, was the divine Son before his birth—and clearly, then, this brings Mary centre stage. In other words, in earthly terms, Jesus was 'always' Son of God—his earthly origin, through Mary, is God's action.

This is further confirmation that it is not in fact possible to discuss Mary's role outside Christological concerns. Indeed, as John Macquarrie states, the doctrine of the virgin birth of Jesus is much more significant for Christology than for any other theological concern (*Mary for all Christians*, T & T Clark, 2001). Theologically, what Luke is stressing is that the birth of Jesus, through Mary, is indeed a redemptive act of God, the creation of a new humanity or even the recreation of a true humanity. His aim is to show that from the time of his earthly existence Jesus was recognised and confessed by his followers as the Son of God. For him, that begins even before his birth with the appearance of the angel to Mary. Note, though, that the angel does not proclaim to Mary the actual incarnation of the eternal Son of God, but announces that the child that she brings into the world 'will be great, and will be called the Son of the Most High, and the Lord God will give to him the throne of his ancestor David' (Luke 1:32).

Matthew, Luke and Mary

Both evangelists, therefore, represent Mary as the only human being associated with the birth of Jesus and as such bestow upon her a unique and central role to play in God's work of salvation. Implicitly, both Matthew and Luke recognise her as a pre-eminent player in the events leading up to Jesus' birth but also give her a crucial role in the emergence of the new community—even a new humanity. I believe that here we reach the real crux of the matter: both evangelists, but maybe particularly Luke, place the story of the role of Mary at the birth in a context that centralises the thrust of the Christian gospel. Here we see what Macquarrie calls the 'transvaluation of all values' and the reversal of the commonly accepted value system. In Mary's time, as in our own, profit, power and status were the order of the day but with those events in Nazareth and later in Bethlehem all of that was changed. Power, profit and status are replaced by love, meekness and respect—and here again we come across the real 'stuff' of liberation and transfiguration.

Luke begins his story of God's redemptive work on earth with a child and a young girl in a dirty stable and brings it to a climax with a humiliated man hanging on a cross bearing the sins and struggles of the whole world. In one of his reflections on the accounts of the virginal birth of Jesus, Rowan Williams also brings us to God's redemptive mission in and through this (*Open to Judgement*, DLT, 1994). He states that the real miracle of Nazareth and Bethlehem was 'the fact of Jesus himself' and that in this 'fact' we see the beginnings of the good news of God's creative and redeeming work being set free in the world. Further, in it we see also the beginnings of all people being called and drawn into a full and fulfilling intimacy with the generosity of Bethlehem's birth.

Beyond Gospel claims

Despite Gospel accounts, credal statements, Christian devotion, religious experience and ongoing spiritual reflection, there are many people for whom any suggestion of the literal virgin birth or conception of Jesus remains at the very least unnecessary—even an anathema. A variety of alternative theories to explain the birth of Jesus have been offered over the years. Some say that Mary did have sexual intercourse with Joseph or even with someone else before marriage or that a Roman soldier called Panthera had raped her. For me such speculation misses the point, which is less about biology and much more about theology and the intimate relationship between God and his people. Biological investigation into the birth of Jesus makes no contribution to the question why a young Jewish woman became symbolically identified with some of the richest liturgical and spiritual traditions of the church. Of course, this is not to say that searching the evidence for clues as to how Mary lived in first-century Palestine is not a worthwhile practice, as such research continues to offer valuable insights into the world into which Jesus was born.

Indeed, in its claim that God entered the world in and through the womb of Mary the Christian tradition must take both the idea and the events of history seriously because it invests the material circumstances of human existence with ultimate significance. To say that a young virgin girl conceived and became the means by which God in Jesus entered the world cannot simply remain a myth—it is a historical claim. From its outset, Christianity has given her a central place in its understanding of the person of Jesus Christ and in its own mission to the world, closely identifying the motherhood of the church with Mary's motherhood of Jesus. To include her in the central discussions concerning the person of Jesus is not an optional extra for Christians, whatever their tradition and denomination. Mary is the linchpin to understanding correctly one of the most crucial doctrines of the Christian tradition, namely, the incarnation.

Against heresies

The Church has recognised this fact from its very beginnings and particularly during those times when it had to defend strenuously both the humanity and divinity of Jesus during various theological controversies. One of the earliest debates surrounded claims made by Nestorius in the year 451. Nestorius was appointed Bishop of Constantinople by the Emperor Theodosius II in 428 and, as bishop, he proclaimed himself a great upholder of Christian orthodoxy. One of the titles associated with Mary at that time was *Theotokos*—Godbearer or Mother of God—and as such was criticised by one of Nestorius' priests. When Nestorius supported that priest, a huge controversy ensued around the appropriate use of this particular title. Basically, Nestorius advocated the idea that there were two separate persons in the incarnate Christ—one divine and one human—as opposed to the orthodox doctrine that the incarnate Christ was one single whole person and thus both fully God and fully man. Eventually the controversy led to the emperor calling a council for the entire church at Ephesus in the year 431 at which the title *Theotokos* was made an official title for Mary.

As well as their message, which had a particular liberating appeal for those on the margins of society (women, slaves, the poor), one of the most important ingredients of the Church's defence of the divine nature of Christ was the church leaders' ability to converse adequately with their detractors. The early Christians were keen to present a robust theology in favour of Christ's divinity, especially in the face of the many pagan philosophies of the day. They were anxious to develop ways to argue that the story of Christ fulfilled and substantiated any philosophy claiming that there was in fact an intimate relationship between matter, spirit, divinity and humanity. Much of the ancient world found it conceptually impossible to imagine God becoming man, God entering flesh, God revealing himself in a Trinity or a virgin becoming a mother.

A new creation in Christ

Clearly Christians are able to make strong claims that Mary, as the mother of Jesus, is in a very deep sense the first person of a new creation in Christ. As such, she stands as a symbol of transfiguration and enables each one of us to begin imagining what it is like to be invited into a world that has rid itself of violence, death and injustice. This is a world where the cosmic battle has been won, the powers of darkness have been conquered and where love triumphs supremely. In Mary, as this first person, an amazing intimacy between God and his people is formed in Christ, and, in the creation of that intimacy, an infinite distance between God and his people has been eternally overcome. In this sense, what I find particularly striking about Christian teaching surrounding the incarnation is that, through it, time reaches a particular fullness. In that fullness we come to recognise a powerful reconciliation of the transience of human existence and the intransience of God's existence. While this is true of the incarnation, it is potentially so for all those 'incarnation moments' in everyday human life. It is when we recognise those 'incarnation moments'—occasions when God's abundance touches our own lives—that we can enter into a more splendid and transfigured life.

God in Christ, born of the virgin Mary, offers us a way of realising how it is, in the experience of Christ's sharing human birth, that he comes close to us and willingly enters into a relationship with men and women. So much of this is also beyond the normal ability to reason but it focuses on 'the place'—the interface—where the power of God and human faith come together in a new creation and where transfiguration can occur. The Anglican theologian A.M. Allchin captured this beautifully when he said that the marvellous interchange which the incarnation brings about could not be more clearly expressed than in this: his descent into our human life that we might be raised into the divine life (*The Joy of all Creation*, DLT, 1983). He continues: 'From the annunciation to Mary to the growth of the Church, all is one action of the grace of God. The theme of deification, our being made God by grace, takes its true place at the heart of Christian teaching.' Mary reminds us of all this, for she is the one who, by her very existence, tells us that the Word has become flesh and has entered into all the common processes of birth and growth. At the very heart of this vision of humanity being invited to become part of God's life and so to carry certain incarnation responsibilities for God's creation, through which all creation can discover transfiguration, Mary has a vital role to play. In her, humanity and divinity communicated and shared in a truly amazing way.

But there still remains a paradox

I was first introduced to some of the issues surrounding the church's teaching on the incarnation through the writings of D.M. Baillie, a 20th-century Scottish theologian. In expounding his theological method, Baillie refers constantly to the great paradoxes of the Christian faith—the paradox of creation, the paradox of providence, the paradox of grace and even the paradox of the incarnation. His basic claim is that in one sense the mystery of God in Christ must always remain a mystery. However, that does not mean that nothing at all can be said about the nature of what is called the 'hypostatic union'—that is, the union of a distinct human personality and the divine personality in Christ. That would be tantamount to confessing that we don't know what we mean when we speak of God being incarnate in Jesus and completely confusing any way of talking about the Trinity. In reading some of Baillie's writings, I have come to recognise that it is, in fact, the incarnation that presents us with the supreme paradox and it is quite possible that we will never be able to eliminate that sense of paradox from it without losing the incarnation itself.

Interestingly, I think there is an element of paradox running right through all religious thinking and theological reflection, primarily because God cannot be comprehended fully by using mere human words or through the categories of our sometimes very inadequate and finite thinking. There is also a danger of falling back too readily on accepting the idea of paradox at face value, as it could make authentic theological reflection an impossible task. What we need to try to do is to maintain a healthy sense of tension between the two sides of every paradox, which can help to drive us back again and again to our primary sources, the immediate utterances of faith found in the scriptures and in the early Christian traditions. Thus, no theological paradox can be justified unless it can be shown to spring directly from those primary sources. Since any paradox is a self-contradictory statement, we simply don't know what it means or what we mean by it unless it has a direct connection with the faith or teaching it seeks to address.

So the essence of theological paradox lies in the reality that all the goodness in men and women does not actually belong to them but rather to God. The paradox comes to the fore when we then admit that in ascribing all our personal goodness to God, we do not actually abrogate human personality nor disclaim personal responsibility. Human goodness is never more truly, freely and fully personal than when men and women are able and willing to say 'not me but God', which, in itself, is stepping further towards a transfigured life. For Baillie, it was the paradox of grace that offered the best clue to understanding the essence of incarnation. The paradox of grace reflects that perfect union of God and humanity at the heart of the incarnation (*God was in Christ*, Faber and Faber, 1948).

The Gospels show that Jesus Christ—the man in whom God chose to become incarnate through Mary—refused to claim anything for himself and ascribed all goodness to God. They also illustrate that Christ desired nothing more than that others might be caught up into the same close union with God. And then those who enter into that same deep and lasting union with God will be able to say in a transfigured way: 'not me but God'. This emphasises humanity's complete dependence on God but also allows men and women to remain themselves; they become wholly dependent on God without the annihilation of who they truly are.

As well as being paradoxical, an authentic Christian interpretation of the incarnation brings us right back to the counter-cultural nature of Christianity. That God willingly opts to become a man in Christ, through Mary, is itself a statement that completely transcends all 'natural' morality. In a sense Christian ethics per se—rules of what we should and should not do—is no longer required. Rather, the incarnational way of doing things drives men and women away from self and towards God, where a distinctive kind of goodness, which can never be achieved through one's own moral endeavour, is allowed to blossom. This is the paradoxical secret, which, while it transcends all ethical behaviour in the way it ascribes goodness to God, does not and should never make us ethically irresponsible. It is the heart of the paradox of the incarnation—human beings are not puppets but responsible people and never more truly personal than in those moments when they are most dependent upon God. Whatever goodness is revealed in human lives, God is there even before that goodness. Herein lies the deepest paradox of the Christian experience and its source is found in the Nazareth/Bethlehem events, when, through Mary, God opted willingly and lovingly to become human in Christ.

Still liberation... but tinged with more paradox

I have already mentioned Gebara and Bingemar, the two South American women theologians who have greatly influenced my thinking on Mary in relation to liberation theology. In an essay on Mary and the liberation model, they pick up on how the question of her virginity can also be interpreted through a liberation lens ('Mary' in Ignacio Ellacuria and Jon Sobrino, editors, *Mysterium Liberationis*, Orbis, 1993). For Jews, virginity had no intrinsic value—virginity was synonymous with being sterile and with the inability to use the greatest gift God had bestowed on women, procreation. In a first-century Palestinian setting, sterility would probably have attracted contempt and so the idealisation of virginity was in itself paradoxical. Gebara and Bingemar make the point that the chain of Jesus' genealogy undergoes a radical break to give way to the Holy Spirit, who, they say, 'invades history with a creative breath and makes life spring where it would naturally be impossible'. This act of divine incarnation, through Mary, regards Jesus' emergence from her womb as the fertile seed of a new people formed by the Spirit. As such, Mary becomes the first and supreme symbol of that new people.

Gebara and Bingemar recognise something radically defining in this act—for them, it throws light on an important anthropological question of what it means to be human. Being human is just like being a virgin, they suggest. It means being 'unexplored' and 'new'. Ideally, what should happen in any 'new and virginal' situation—as happened to Mary—is that God is formed in the 'womb' or in the heart of that situation. Mary's virginity, fertilised by the Holy Spirit, corresponds to the vocation of all men and women to be an open and willing dwelling place for those in need, which is pure liberation theology! This brings us back to the paradox of the incarnation in the sense that Mary's virginity becomes a metaphor for all men and women's inability to accomplish wholeness and salvation without God's grace. Mary's virginity is a sign of total surrender to the God of authentic living. Gebara and Bingemar put this in terms of Mary's virginity being 'a total abandonment to the death-dealing idols of contemporary society—that culture of death and despair felt by so many—and becoming a sign to all men and women who choose to tread the path of Jesus and live the reality of his kingdom'.

For me, the climax of any reflection on Mary's virginity must lie in the way it reveals God's omnipotent glory in the poor, the powerless and those despised by the affluent world. Virginity, not in itself enormously prized in Mary's day, is the chosen location of God's dwelling place on earth. God's preference for the poor and the despised of the world becomes explicit when that 'preference' becomes the place in which the creative and redeeming God chooses to make his home, in Mary's womb.

Always pointing us to Christ

In my journey through this vast area of Mary's intimate relationship with God and her virginity I have learned an important fact: that, on the whole (and there are, of course, numerous exceptions), sensible and clear-thinking Christians do recognise that Mary always points towards Christ. I have heard it said too often that Catholics 'worship' Mary even more than they do Jesus himself. I have not found this to be the case. As I have already said, to study Mary means always to study Christ, and to study Christ means asking questions about how it all relates to us in our daily lives. But any conversation about how that relationship happens is often determined by human experience in particular places and at particular times. Time and context are crucial. Theological reflection is always conditioned by socio-cultural realities and our attempts at making sense of these are usually expressed by metaphors and images based on the interaction between, on the one hand, our sense of God and, on the other, our human experiences in particular places and at particular times. The way we describe God—and our experience of the divine—in truth affects the way we define ourselves as we are made in the image of God. While this human/divine interaction is found in all spheres of theological thinking and teaching, it is, I believe, particularly present in our exploration of Mary.

Part 3

Bearer of the incarnation, witness to the resurrection

Over the years I have become increasingly convinced that as we celebrate the great Christian festivals—whether they be the major ones such as Christmas, Easter and Pentecost or some of the others—the important question we need to ask constantly is: 'How does this celebration touch my life?' How do these celebrations make a difference in our lives? In what ways do they challenge us as Christians? Are we affected or changed by what we do at specific religious celebrations? In many ways these are questions to ask on any Sunday in the Christian year: are we the same when we leave our place of worship as when we first arrived? Indeed, is it conceivably possible to spend time with fellow Christians in prayer, in worship, in song, in listening to God's word as revealed in scripture and not in some way, however small, be changed, be different, be made new? For if the claims Christians make about God's mighty acts in creation are true, then we can only be changed—we can only be renewed and refreshed in our relationship with God and with each other.

Christmas and Easter: kingdom hinges

One of the gifts of journeying through the Christian year is the constant, rhythmical opportunity to retrace not only the pathways through the life, ministry, death and resurrection of Jesus Christ but also through our own lives in relation to those pathways—that's what true pilgrimage means. Year after year, Sunday after Sunday, festival after festival Christians keep getting new opportunities to wrestle with those searching questions about how we allow ourselves to be challenged and changed by the life of Christ. Two significant 'hinges' hold that Christian year firmly in place: the incarnation (Christmas) and the resurrection (Easter), both hinges signifying the reality of the kingdom that was inaugurated in and through the person of Jesus Christ.

In relation to these events, 'kingdom' does not simply mean 'kingdom values', as if imitating such qualities as the compassion and love and tolerance and self-sacrifice of Jesus is enough—as crucial as such qualities are. Rather, by using 'kingdom' in this context, the 'good news' challenge us to dig deeper in our understanding of what it means to say that the kingdom of God was brought to us in and through the incarnation and the resurrection. Christmas and Easter do not simply ask Christians to gaze at the manger or ponder the cross but rather to recognise that they point us in the direction of a God who has opted to become very close to us at every level in this life.

Incarnation, the very heartbeat of God

There is no doubt that the incarnation of God in Jesus Christ constitutes the very heartbeat of the Christian faith. During the best part of 1700 years theologians of all Christian traditions have passionately debated what the doctrine of the incarnation really means. It is a statement that God himself, without ceasing to be God, came to share human life, not just in but as a particular man, at a particular time and in a particular place. The human life that Jesus lived and the death he died are believed to have been the human life and death of God himself. This is what is meant by the Nicene creed's statement that Jesus Christ was truly God as well as being truly man. Incarnation is not only concerned with the beginnings of the good news but also directly related to the cross and resurrection—we cannot accept one without the other.

A belief in Christ rooted in incarnation demands that we read the events of both the beginning and the end of his earthly life as two parts of a single narrative and this implies the strict uniqueness of Jesus in the narrative. If God becomes man, this happens only once, because to be human means to have just one human life, in a particular place and at a particular time. The Christian tradition also profoundly affirms that God in Christ subjected himself to the world's evil at its most harsh and cruel and, by doing so, both revealed his love and accepted responsibility for the crucifixion. It was not possible for this to be done indirectly, through a representative. There is an immense difference between expressing sympathy with suffering and actually bearing the suffering oneself. The point about God taking responsibility for Christ's death and consequently the world's evil depends wholly on the incarnation.

From this comes the reality that being a Christian gives no easy escape from suffering. Christians ask the same questions as those without any kind of faith and are no better at answering them! The Christian, however, believes that God knows the answers because of his presence in Christ—the Christ who himself knew the night of dereliction which 'murdered God' and sought to kill life's very meaning. Christ is God with us, and into whatever depths of suffering we may sink, God has been there before us. We cannot talk of the death of Jesus as the supreme manifestation of the self-sacrificing love of God without a firm belief in the incarnation. Without the incarnation, God would not be sacrificing himself: he would be demanding that his human representative be the one who gives the supreme example of what self-sacrifice means.

Incarnation gives substance and guarantee to the belief that God is eternally and essentially love. The most that a non-incarnational form of Christianity can say is that the human Jesus certainly believed in and himself experienced the love of God, and that he also enabled his followers to experience God in this way—perhaps for many centuries afterwards. But suppose that all these experiences are just one aspect of some sort of experiment that God is conducting with the whole human race as his experimental animals. Suppose he was trying to find out, at this stage in his experiment, how human beings would behave if he treated them in the way that they themselves describe as 'loving'. What if he has now decided to try some quite different treatment? What if he has begun to do so already? Perhaps the theologians who once claimed that 'God is dead' were simply signalling this change in the conditions of the experiment. Perhaps the threat of nuclear extinction is another indication that the conditions of the experiment have changed.

It is only by believing in Christ and his incarnation that we are fully equipped with a defence against the fearful possibility of such thinking. Incarnational Christology states that the relationship that is seen to exist between Christ and God is a revelation of the eternal relationship of love that constitutes the very essence of the being of God. This is seen most clearly in John's Gospel, where Christ is seen as the eternal Son, God's only begotten, who is loved by the Father from before the foundation of the world. The human life of Jesus is regarded by John as a projection of this eternal relationship of love upon the field of time. John's claim that this historical figure is God the Son Incarnate means that the relation of mutual love which exists between himself and God the Father is an accurate representation of the very being and essence of the Godhead. God is shown to be a supremely personal God whose nature and whose name is love. He is not some transcendent mastermind who creates us simply to experiment with us.

Mary, the new ark of the covenant

Mary, as the immediate source of this new human existence—the bearer of the incarnation—has a unique role to play. We have already seen in Chapter 1 how the language used to portray Mary in the Gospels echoes much Old Testament imagery. Following their entry into the promised land, and in order to preserve unity, the Hebrew people carried their most treasured possession in an ark, which represented for them the essence of God's presence. Eventually, David brought the ark to the city of Jerusalem and he leapt and danced before it, celebrating that this symbol of God had come to him (2 Samuel 6:5). Similarly, the unborn John the Baptist leapt in Elizabeth's womb when she heard Mary's greeting and realised that the mother of the Messiah had come to her (Luke 1:41). For Jewish people the temple became the ultimate dwelling place of God. In the same spirit Mary carried a new treasure in her womb—the sign and seal of God's new relationship with his people—and by doing this she herself can be seen as becoming a new ark of the covenant. As the bearer of the incarnation Mary ensures that God's presence returns to his people.

Although Mary is not mentioned at every stage of the Gospel narrative, she still plays a crucial role in the unfolding of the kingdom (as we have already seen). Her prominence becomes apparent at several key moments—the annunciation, the birth of Jesus, Jesus' first miracle, the developing understanding of what it means to be the 'family of Jesus', the death of Jesus and the coming of the Holy Spirit. Too much thinking about Mary merely recalls her sitting in the stable at Bethlehem. It fails to capture her crucial role at the foot of the cross or the importance of her praying with the disciples following the resurrection. Of course Mary was there at the beginning of Jesus' earthly life but she was also very significant at the end.

Reading between the lines of the Gospels, I get the strong impression that on occasions Mary was bewildered, puzzled and not quite fully understanding what was going on. This could well be the case on at least two occasions near the beginning of Luke's Gospel. The first was when Jesus was presented to Simeon in the temple. After the old man had recited his famous words of fulfilment and satisfaction at seeing the Messiah at last, he turned to Mary and prophesied that all of this would give her pain and anguish (Luke 2:33–35). On hearing that she must have wondered what on earth was going on. And as if that was not enough, there was a second occasion when both Mary and Joseph could well have been confused. In the temple, the boy Jesus responded to Mary's worries concerning his whereabouts with words that she just could not fathom (vv. 48–50).

Luke begins his Gospel in the temple where the birth of John the Baptist is foretold, and he concludes it by returning to the temple where the disciples gather to praise God with 'great joy' (24:52–53) The boy Jesus' response to Mary links these two temple experiences, when Luke records the first words of Jesus (2:48–50). No longer do Gabriel or Mary or Zechariah or an angel or Simeon pronounce who Jesus is; Jesus does it himself in his response to Mary. What is particularly appealing about Luke's presentation of the beginning and the ending of Jesus' ministry is its overt humanity. In her reaction to Jesus' presence in the temple Mary shows her humanity—she is the mother of the Lord yet also just like any other mother, worried about her child's safety. Then to counterbalance the significance of his first recorded words (v. 49), Jesus does not perform any great miracle but simply participates in the everyday life of his family (v. 51)—he is the saviour of the world but also just like any other boy. Mary and Joseph never quite understood that their son's relationship to God took precedence over his relationship to them—could this be part of the piercing 'sword' spoken of by Simeon (v. 35)? Whatever the mix of normality and divinity is in this passage, Mary continued her journey of faith right through to the end and probably never stopped pondering in her heart the true meaning and destiny of her son and her part in this extraordinary train of events.

In the next two chapters I want to explore the significance of Mary's role at the beginning and at the end of Jesus' earthly life. I have already highlighted how crucial the traditions surrounding the incarnation and resurrection are to the whole Christian story—not only are these the very hinges that hold the story together but they also reveal the quintessential thrust of the kingdom of God. Christians need to read the incarnation and the resurrection together and Mary is central to both.

What is also interesting is that as the bearer of the incarnation Mary was someone of no real human importance—she had no legal standing; she was not from a prominent tribe; she did not lead a family; she was a girl on the edge of everything. The dignity and power of the incarnation came from an 'edge place'. It is this idea of 'power coming from the edge' that is my guiding principle in Chapters 5 and 6. I want to explore this idea at two levels. Firstly, as I have already mentioned, Mary herself was a person who was at the edge of everything—status, gender, age, family, reputation—and yet she was supremely chosen to be the bearer of the incarnation. Secondly, and deeply connected to my emphasis on the importance of reading incarnation and resurrection (Christmas and Easter) together, Mary comes into remarkable prominence at the beginning of the Gospel—the birth of Jesus—and at the end of the Gospel—the death of Jesus. Both places, the stable and the cross, are themselves quintessentially 'edge places'.

Edge places can also be described as 'liminal' or threshold places—places that transgress the limits of culture, language and personal boundaries by which lives are normally framed and controlled. Certain places have the power to 'strip one bare' and reduce people to their essential simplicity—no clutter, no distraction. In these places routine and usual dependencies cease and the new experience of the edge offers something that is new, even if a little dangerous and risky. This is what attracted many early Christians to seek

God in a closer way in the wilderness and the desert. By venturing towards the 'edge' they were able to forge a way forward into something utterly beyond previously conceived limits of being. Such 'edge places' allowed them to be truly attentive to God's voice and his revealing of himself.

Mountain-top experiences

In the Gospel of Matthew these 'edge places' are often mountains or hills and he actually builds his whole drama as a journey from a mountain (of temptation in Matthew 4), where Jesus refuses an easy and familiar way, to a hill (Calvary). Calvary is a declaration to his disciples and quite possibly to his mother as well that all power in heaven and earth has now been given to him.

Between these two particular 'mountains' there are a further four, all of which take on this 'edge' characteristic and thus continue to connect the idea of an 'edge place' with proclaiming the kingdom of God. On one of them, Jesus teaches the new and radical ethic of the true meaning of God's kingdom in the Sermon on the Mount (Matthew 5–7). On another, he prefigures the messianic banquet of the kingdom in the feeding of the 5000 (14:13–21) and on the mount of the transfiguration he anticipates his absolute glory (17:1–8). Then, finally, he describes the time of the coming of the kingdom on the Mount of Olives (24:3). On each of the mountains the recipients of kingdom hope are drawn powerfully to the 'edge' where shape and meaning is given to how their ministry will break down old and tired established world orders. A new compass to lead the way into the kingdom is found, and through it, new rules are adopted. In all these mountain-top experiences the 'edge place' is always risky and different but there is one common feature—those present are invited to enter the unfamiliar. The disciples are constantly being dragged away from home and all those things that offer false security, towards an unexpected, 'edgy' place where they encounter God in a different and unexpected way.

The edge is not only a geographical place, however; it is also a place of the heart and symbolises a call to consider things from a different perspective. This happens often in the Gospels (John 3, in the encounter between Jesus and Nicodemus, for instance). Individuals are called by Jesus and then challenged to go deeper within themselves and to take risks in faith. Indeed, following Jesus as a disciple was itself a risk of faith—it still is! I've often wondered whether this is what Jesus really meant when he told his disciples to go into 'another room' to pray—possibly, it was not one with four walls but the inner 'room' that lies within each person where depth of meaning, authenticity and truthfulness can be discovered. Discovering such personal 'edge places' can also save us from superficiality and mediocrity; they can help us to move on from frustration and even despair to a place of true value and integrity. In such movement dreams can be enlivened, feelings activated, yearnings fulfilled and freedom achieved.

In Chapters 5 and 6 I therefore seek to revisit Mary's own 'edge place' encounters: firstly, in Nazareth, where by saying a totally risky 'yes' to God she becomes the bearer of the incarnation. That 'yes' proved to be even more risky than she could have ever imagined as, secondly, this 'yes' took her to the foot of the cross, where she became a witness to the resurrection.

Chapter 5

Light shining from Nazareth

In the sixth month the angel Gabriel was sent by God to a town in Galilee called Nazareth, to a virgin engaged to a man whose name was Joseph, of the house of David. The virgin's name was Mary. And he came to her and said, 'Greetings, favoured one! The Lord is with you.' But she was much perplexed by his words and pondered what sort of greeting this might be. The angel said to her, 'Do not be afraid, Mary, for you have found favour with God. And now, you will conceive in your womb and bear a son, and you will name him Jesus. He will be great, and will be called the Son of the Most High, and the Lord God will give to him the throne of his ancestor David. He will reign over the house of Jacob for ever, and of his kingdom there will be no end.' Mary said to the angel, 'How can this be, since I am a virgin?' The angel said to her, 'The Holy Spirit will come upon you, and the power of the Most High will overshadow you; therefore the child to be born will be holy; he will be called Son of God. And now, your relative Elizabeth in her old age has also conceived a son; and this is the sixth month for her who was said to be barren. For nothing will be impossible with God.' Then Mary said, 'Here am I, the servant of the Lord; let it be with me according to your word.' Then the angel departed from her.

LUKE 1:26–38

Luke's account of the angel's annunciation of the birth of Jesus to Mary contains seven specific traditions, all of which are also mentioned in Matthew's Gospel:

- Mary is a virgin and is engaged to Joseph but they have not yet come to live together (Luke 1:27, 34; 2:5; Matthew 1:18)
- Joseph is from the house of David (Luke 1:27; 2:4; Matthew 1:16, 20)
- An angel from heaven announces the coming birth of Jesus (Luke 1:28–30; Matthew 1:20–21)
- Jesus himself is said to be a son of David (Luke 1:32; Matthew 1:1)
- Jesus' conception will happen through the power of the Holy Spirit (Luke 1:35; Matthew 1:18, 20)
- Joseph plays no part in the conception of Jesus (Luke 1:34–35; Matthew 1:18–25)
- The name 'Jesus' is given in heaven before the actual birth (Luke 1:31; Matthew 1:21).

Matthew for Joseph and Luke for Mary

Although Matthew and Luke share these seven specific traditions surrounding the birth of Jesus, as we saw in Chapter 2, they differ quite significantly in their overall presentation of the birth and especially, perhaps, in relation to Mary.

In the first two chapters of Matthew's Gospel, Joseph is mentioned eight times and Mary three times, and in Luke's Gospel we discover the opposite as in his first two chapters Mary is mentioned eleven times and Joseph three times.

Matthew seems to be absolutely determined to portray the whole life of Jesus as the fulfilment of Old Testament prophecies. In this sense he was probably keen to present his birth narrative in such a way that it resonated with traditional Old Testament birth stories, such as the birth of Samson (Judges 13). Although the angel directly appeared on more than one occasion to Samson's mother, it is Manoah—Samson's father—who actually plays the central role in the events surrounding Samson's birth. Similarly, Matthew records an angelic annunciation to Joseph (1:18–23) but not to Mary (compare Luke's account). As with his birth narrative, Matthew's evolving agenda places a great deal of prominence on other Old Testament traditions: Jesus is the new David born in Bethlehem (Matthew 2:5/Micah 5:2–3); Jesus is the Immanuel and stands amongst his people as the very presence of God (Matthew 1:23/Isaiah 7:14).

On the other hand, Mary is at the centre of Luke's political and liberating agenda—he is keen to challenge the political structures of the day and as such portrays Jesus as the one who brings liberation to those on the edge, the *anawim*. Luke wants his Gospel to embrace the whole world—a world way beyond the confines of Judaism. Indeed, as the Anglican biblical scholar N.T. Wright points out, even Luke's emphasis on the census is significant in this respect (*The Meaning of Jesus*, SPCK, 1999). The census took place at a time of political rebellion, and by relating Jesus' birth directly to the census, Luke roots Jesus' life and ministry in a kingdom movement that constantly and radically challenges any moves to persecute, isolate or stigmatise. By presenting his account of the nativity from the perspective of Mary—a woman in a man's world—Luke makes a powerful statement that signals the dawn of a new age for all those who may be different; now is their time of transfiguration.

However, despite the differences between Matthew and

Luke, there is one overwhelmingly significant commonality—that both Mary and Joseph said 'yes' to the angel. For the rest of this chapter I want to focus on the implications of Mary's 'yes' and to explore the way in which her response was the first ray of brightness that shone from Nazareth—a transfiguring and liberating light.

A yes from Mary and a yes from Jesus

When I begin to consider the wider implications of Mary's 'yes', I'm aware that at the incarnation of Jesus two conversations were happening, which go together and blend into one. The first conversation is the one that took place between Mary and the angel when Mary says 'yes': 'Here am I, the servant of the Lord; let it be with me according to your word' (Luke 1:38). As I ponder this episode, I am reminded of another experience that parallels Mary's 'yes' in which a second conversation takes place, but this time between the Father and the Son—a conversation which actually sets the incarnation in motion. In this second dialogue the Son says to the Father: 'Sacrifices and offerings you have not desired, but a body you have prepared for me; in burnt offerings and sin offerings you have taken no pleasure. Then I said, "See, God, I have come to do your will, O God"' (Hebrews 10:5–7). In this conversation the words of Psalm 40:7–8 are attributed to Christ at his incarnation. Psalm 40 insists that God much prefers obedience to sacrifices; it is not a repudiation of ritual but a direct statement of its relative inferiority. Since Jesus' obedience was expressed by his willing offering of his body—himself—in death, the words 'Here I am' (Psalm 40:7) are peculiarly applicable to him. God's preferring of obedience to sacrifice is interpreted as his repudiation of Old Testament sacrifices and their replacement by the self-offering of Jesus. In the two conversations the 'yes' of the Son and the 'yes' of Mary—a double 'yes'—become a single 'yes' and thus the 'Word becomes flesh' in Mary.

In this double 'yes', the obedience of the Son becomes truly embodied, and by her own 'yes', Mary physically gives him that body. Ultimately, what each has to do with the other is found in this double 'yes' and it is this that results in the incarnation. The Son's answer directs us to this point of profound unity and it is precisely to this that Jesus points his mother. Here, in their common 'yes' to the will of the Father, an answer is found. In a sense, this sheds light on Jesus' words in another episode between him and Mary, when he says 'my hour has not yet come' (John 2:4). Jesus never acts completely alone, and never for the sake of pleasing those around him—not even his mother! The Father is always the starting point of his actions, and this is what unites him to Mary, because she wishes to make her request in this same unity of will with the Father. And so, surprisingly, after hearing Jesus' answer to her at the wedding party in Galilee, which seems to refuse her original request for more wine, she can only say to the servants, 'Do whatever he tells you' (John 2:5). Jesus is not a wonder worker and does not play games with his power in what is, after all, a private family wedding.

Pushing love to the utmost

What Jesus does do, though, is to offer a sign in which he proclaims his hour, the hour of the wedding feast, the hour of union between God and all humanity. He does not merely 'make' wine but transforms the human wedding feast into an image of the divine wedding feast, to which the Father invites all people through the Son and in which he gives everyone an abundance of wine—liberation and transfiguration. So the wedding feast becomes an image of that moment when Jesus pushes love to the utmost, allowing his body to be rent asunder and thus giving himself as the ultimate liberation, having become completely one with all of humanity—a transfiguring marriage between God and people. Thus, a momentary need is resolved in a truly divine manner and the initial request is superabundantly granted. Jesus' 'hour' has not yet arrived, but in the sign of water changed into wine, in the sign of this festive gift, he even now anticipates that 'hour'. Of course, Jesus' real 'hour' is the cross and his definitive 'hour' will be his return to this world.

Imagining the incarnation in creative ways

Matthew, Luke and the author of the letter to the Hebrews were clearly imaginative theological thinkers, certainly as far as their reflections on the incarnation—the mystery of God becoming man in the person of Jesus Christ—is concerned.

It is exciting to see how these writers (and others) were bold enough to use images and symbols that conveyed this deep mystery in creative and imaginative ways. That imaginative creativity did not stop with the New Testament, but continued in many early Christian writings and thinking, indeed into the present day. As such it raises the question as to whether we are bold enough to explore through that same imaginative creativity the power of the eternal Word becoming flesh through Mary and dwelling in our midst—'pitching his tent' alongside ours. In truth, seeking such boldness has been a driving force in my own quest into Mary's life and relevance. I firmly believe that it cannot be enough simply to leave grasping the power of the incarnation to what Matthew and Luke and even John had to say. I have a hunch that their variations on the mystery of God becoming human arose from their own constant striving after a clearer grasp of such an infinite concept. Over the course of history their reflections have encouraged others to try again and again to capture the depth of that moment.

One such reflection is the *Protoevangelium* of James (already mentioned in Chapter 1), which is contained in the New Testament Apocrypha, probably written in the middle of the second century. In this, Mary plays a central role. As a document it was known to at least three of the earliest post-New Testament writers—Justin Martyr, Clement of Alexandria and Origen. This is where we are told the names of Mary's parents, Anna and Joachim, and about her own miraculous birth and upbringing in the temple. The document also informs us that by the time of Mary's pregnancy, Joseph was an aged widower with grown-up sons whom he had had with a previous wife. James relates a story about how Joseph was horrified to learn of Mary's pregnancy even to the point of asking her to undergo tests in the temple to check on her virginity. There are also quite clear parallels between this text and the Gospels—the annunciation, the visit to Elizabeth, the magi and the violence of Herod. It also places the birth in a cave and in Chapter 18 of the *Protoevangelium* the author gives Joseph the opportunity to 'speak' for himself! The chapter relates a story in which Joseph, shortly before the birth, goes in search of a midwife, leaving Mary in the cave with one of his sons standing guard.

For me, in this particular story, James captures the real depth of that incarnation moment beautifully when he says: 'Now I, Joseph, was walking about, and yet I was not walking. And I looked up into the vault of heaven, and I saw it standing still, and I looked up into the air, and saw the air in amazement, and the birds of heaven remained motionless. And I looked at the earth, and I saw a dish placed there and workmen lying around it, with their hands in the dish. But those who chewed did not chew, and those who lifted up anything lifted up nothing, and those who put something to their mouth put nothing to their mouth, but all had their faces turned upwards. And behold, sheep were being driven and yet they did not come forward, but stood still; and the shepherd raised his hand to strike them with his staff, but his hand remained up. And I looked at the river, and saw the mouths of the goats over it and they did not drink. And then all at once everything went on its course again' (18:2: *The New Testament Apocrypha,* edited by Wilhelm Schneemelcher, Westminster/John Knox Press, 1991).

The story then continues with Joseph returning with the midwife to the cave only to find that it is completely covered by a cloud. When the cloud is lifted, a pure bright light shines from inside the cave—so bright that those outside are unable to look at it. When the light dims, those gathered there see Mary holding on to her new-born babe, Jesus. With imagination and creativity the *Protoevangelium* underlines that in this birth heaven and earth, time and eternity all became one and the world briefly stood still.

First a cloud, then a light and eventually glory

One of the aspects of Joseph's account of the birth in this story is the way it resonates with other biblical images suggesting that, in those moments of godly encounters, time does indeed stand still and heaven and earth unite as one.

In her own state of transfiguration, Mary was in a sense on fire but she was not consumed—just like the burning bush (Exodus 3:1–6). As Mary became a mother but without losing her virginity, so, figuratively, she bore within herself a flame of fire that eventually became the living God. Interestingly, on Mount Horeb the burning bush was a crucial connecting link between heaven and earth; similarly at the annunciation Mary became that same connecting link. Standing on the very crossroads of the Testaments, Mary, as a kind of new burning bush, was overshadowed by the power of the Most High (Luke 1:35). This 'overshadowing' was, I think, the same cloud that symbolised the veiled presence of God among his people (Exodus 40:16–38). This was the cloud that indicated God's glory—the same cloud that James, in his *Protoevangelium,* imagines to have come over the cave, eventually giving way to a powerful revelation of a divine bright light.

The same glory of God appeared to the Hebrew people in the wilderness in a pillar of cloud and God also spoke to Moses in a cloud. On Mount Tabor, when Jesus himself was transfigured, a cloud once again overshadowed those present and Jesus conversed with Moses and Elijah. From the cloud God declared Jesus as his beloved one and ordered those present to 'listen to him' (Luke 9:35). In the annunciation Mary, too, was overshadowed as she listened to the voice of an angel, recognising possibly that it was the same glory that had overshadowed Moses long before her—the same glory that had filled the tabernacle in the wilderness and later the temple (Isaiah 6:3). Now God's glory was to rest upon Mary, soon to be unveiled and revealed in a way that had never happened before, offering the opportunity for a transfigured life to all God's people. It is not, I think, insignificant that the first chapter of John's Gospel speaks not in terms of 'cloud' but rather in terms of 'light'. The unveiling of God's face that once upon a time could only be encountered through a cloud could now, through the incarnation, be experienced as pure light shining on his people.

Back to the heart of the matter

My journey through some of the imaginative and creative descriptions of what happened around the time of Jesus' birth keeps bringing me back to the question: what exactly happened that day in Nazareth? That, I think, is the heart of the matter. Clearly, Mary had a deep spiritual encounter in which she became very aware of God in a powerful way. My own understanding of this encounter is that God was asking her a question: 'Mary, are you prepared to come on a journey with me? Are you open to doing something very special for me?' Mary's response was: 'Here am I, the servant of the Lord; let it be with me according to your word' (Luke 1:38), in another word, 'Yes'. By imagining the conversation between Mary and God in this way, I don't feel that I am in any way being unfaithful to the unfolding of Luke's interpretation of the 'heart of the matter'. I think that Mary simply puts herself into the hands of God and leaves whatever the future has in store for her firmly in those almighty hands.

In previous chapters I have already mentioned the writings of the Swiss Catholic theologian Hans Urs von Balthasar, who devoted much of his theological explorations to Mary. In one of his commentaries on Balthasar's work, Raymond Gawronski notes that Balthasar uses a particularly interesting German word to translate Mary's 'yes', *Jawort* (*Word and Silence*, T & T Clark, 1995). Gawronski draws our attention to the fact that *Jawort* is far more than simply 'yes'.

It is more akin to the 'I do' that appears in marriage vows. So the implication here may well be that as well as a mother and virgin, Mary is also a 'bride'. Her 'yes' to God is deeper than agreeing simply to do a job or serve a purpose; it is more about her entering a life-long journey alongside God.

Interestingly, there is a powerful sense of obedience surrounding the word *Jawort* and its use here by Balthasar at the beginning of the act of incarnation can remind us, too, of the disobedience of Adam and Eve at the beginning of the act of creation. Mary's 'yes' seems to serve as a complete reversal of that original human disobedience. This is why, in many ways, Mary is often referred to as the new Eve, bridging two Testaments, two epochs, two acts of God's direct intervention in the affairs of the world. Her 'yes' is an agreement through which she accepts all that will inevitably befall her. She willingly enters into a direct, active and cooperative relationship and, by doing so, she is fulfilling something that God has prepared the *anawim* to become. Mary's 'yes' enables and allows God's 'yes' to become real for all men and women—in the person of Jesus, who, as God's 'yes', similarly enables and allows all men and women to enter into a liberating and transfiguring relationship with God.

The Latin American liberation theologians Ivone Gebara and Maria Clara Bingemer see in Mary's 'yes' the same transfiguring possibilities that are available for all God's people. In her agreement to journey with God, Mary prepares a way for men and women of every age to journey with God in open-ended ways. In the moment of incarnation Gebara and Bingemer see clear and hopeful signs of the kingdom—God's kingship becoming manifest in the *anawim*. The kingdom of God will probably not culminate in some mega display of his power but rather be manifest through the ordinary, through the events of love and justice when men and women are prepared to say 'yes' to one another in order to make possible the transfiguration of a severely damaged world.

In truth, God continues to reach out to his people through annunciation—an extraordinary calling lying deep within all that is ordinary in life. In this way, the ordinariness of life stands still long enough for the beam of light to shine and touch the root of all that is authentically human. Contemporary annunciations, as the annunciation to Mary, are always connected with the 'stuff' of real life—they are about recognising and hearing the faithful presence of God in the midst of people who both struggle with and rejoice in life.

God's announcement of love

Inevitably, the idea of a contemporary annunciation—an encounter between God and people today—acquires a sharper focus when it is linked to suffering or pain. It is in this way that an annunciation can become, on the one hand, a liberation from a sense of alienation and, on the other, an opportunity to reach a transfigured existence. This is how, in the case of Mary, the annunciation was for her both joyous and tragic—it encompassed life and death, birth and cross, Nazareth and Calvary. It was inevitable, as has been already stated, that Gabriel's annunciation to Mary would lead her directly to the foot of the cross. In the next chapter I will explore the anguish Mary must have experienced there but to end this chapter I want to show how Mary's experiences at the start and at the end of Jesus' earthly life are inexorably connected and cannot be understood in isolation.

In one of his Holy Week addresses Lindsay McKenna, an Anglican priest working in London, said, 'We all know the story of the annunciation, but we tend to tell it in the light of Mary's response. Think of it for our purposes at the moment rather in terms of God's arrival on the scene, in the person of the angel Gabriel. Here is God's announcement of love: not so much Mary's love of God, but God's love of Mary, or rather, of the people whom Mary represents—a people who for thousands of years have had such an on/off relationship with their God. They are a wayward people to whom God now says: I am ready now, you are ready now, in the presence of this virgin girl, to receive the greatest gift of all and to attain the salvation you long for. That salvation is achieved, of course, in the passion which we celebrate this week. The part we play in our own salvation is to acknowledge and accept the great love of God for us' (preached in St Andrew's Church, Catford, Holy Week 2013).

Lindsay McKenna manages to crystallise not only the way in which Nazareth, as the physical place of annunciation, and Calvary, as the actual place of the cross, are connected, but that it is in fact not possible to make real sense of one without the other.

Carols of the Welsh *plygain*

In my own native Welsh tradition there is another ancient custom that brings this same intimacy between Nazareth and Calvary to the fore. Since medieval times Christians have gathered in various parts of Wales (more especially in rural Wales) to sing what are known in Welsh as *carolau y plygain*, the carols of *plygain*. To translate *plygain* is not a straightforward task. Although it can sometimes be translated as simply 'early morning', in reality it is much more than that. It is about the first light of morning, the dawn with its shining and hopeful light, even the time of the cock crow. So, in the wee small hours as the light gradually strengthens, Welsh Christians, even to this day, gather after Christmas to sing a particular Welsh genre of carols. This genre demands that the singing must happen after Christmas because the carols cannot ever anticipate the birth of Jesus, and that they are always to be sung unaccompanied, thus adding something to the particular experience that they seek to convey—one of deep mystery. The intentional heart of the *plygain* carols is that they consistently link the birth of Jesus Christ with his death—none of them celebrates the one without the other. In a very determined way they are saying that it is impossible to make sense of Christmas without Holy Week and Easter.

Traditionally, on the whole, Wales has always done its work of theology through poetry and hymns as opposed to large tomes written by professional theologians and this is to be seen almost at its best in the *plygain* carols. As well as their particular genre, these carols enshrine some of the most sophisticated Welsh theology surrounding the birth and death of Jesus—incarnation and salvation. There are hundreds of these carols preserved in several collections. Allow me to share just three examples.

One of the best known is *Ar Gyfer Heddiw'r Bore*, literally 'In Readiness for Today's Morning' as opposed simply to being ready for *this* morning. The carol contains four powerful verses that trace the life of Jesus from his birth, through his years with Mary, to the crown of thorns and ultimately to the washing away of our sins through the cross. However, it is the first two verses that I find particularly enthralling.

The first of these opens with the title line *Ar Gyfer Heddiw'r Bore* and informs us that it was the reality of Christ's birth that made us ready for 'today's morning'. The carol then goes on trace the birth of Christ from its very beginnings, emphasising four significant events: that the child comes from the root of Jesse; that he carries the whole strength of Bosra; that he contains the law of Sinai; and that he is the atonement of Calvary. Mention is then made that on Mary's lap the child who was all of this took milk from her breast. The second verse goes on to sing vividly of how the personified life-giving prophecies of Ezekiel and Daniel also now sit on Mary's lap. The verse also describes Mary as one bearing the child of three promises: the promised child of Isaiah, the promise of life given to Adam, and the promise that in Christ we encounter the alpha and the omega.

Another of the *plygain* carols is known as *Carol Wil Cae Coch*, which translated means 'the carol of Wil of the Red Field'. Presumably, Wil, the abbreviated name for William, was the author who lived in a house called the 'Red Field', and this shows that, despite their theological sophistication, on the whole these carols were composed by ordinary Christians doing what was natural—expressing their faith in God through singing. The first two verses of this carol proclaim in very strong terms that the child born in Bethlehem was truly the 'Lord of Lords' and 'King of Kings' promised by Isaiah. Having left the throne of the Father, the Saviour of the world now rests in a manger in sheer and utter humility. Then the carol, like so many others in this tradition, traces the lineage of Jesus directly back to heaven. It also takes a forward glance and points us towards the end of time, stating that, in Christ, divinity wears the cloak of humanity so as to purge away all sin and rid the world of evil.

Finally, there is *Carol Eliseus*, which translated means 'Elijah's Carol' and it is worth bearing in mind that in Welsh Eliseus is a common name, more so than Elijah is in

English. This carol begins by asking people what they can hear and what they feel at this time of year. The answer is then provided: the bells of Jerusalem, as opposed to the bells of Bethlehem, and we have a feeling of mourning but a mourning that leads to the promise of a new dawn.

The second two verses of this carol bring us right back to the crux of the annunciation and beg us to ask the question who it is that really lies in the manger of Bethlehem. Again, the answer comes: immortality of a unique kind. On the heel of the first question comes a second question: who can possibly recognise the tenderness and graciousness of this child in the manger? The answer is interesting for it suggests that, despite the annunciation, not even Gabriel can fully recognise the child of this sacred manger—what has happened is too big and glorious to be defined at a moment's glance. Then a third question is asked: who can this child, wrapped in swaddling clothes, possibly be? Again, the answer comes: this is none other than eternity itself. As in so many of these *plygain* carols, this eternity comes to us through Mary in order to lift humanity from the dirge of sin. The carols are united in their proclamation that one day Jesus Christ will be fully recognised but only when the cloud is lifted and the bright light allowed to shine in order to reveal the truth of the manger—that in it lay the Messiah.

Earlier in this chapter I advocated a creative and imaginative approach to the events surrounding the birth of Jesus, trying to grasp the truth of them, just as Matthew and Luke did, while of course remaining faithful to the original witness of the Gospels. My feeling is that the *plygain* carols do this rather beautifully and they also provide an impressive bridge across which we are able to move from Nazareth to Jerusalem.

Chapter 6

Anguish at the foot of the cross

Meanwhile, standing near the cross of Jesus were his mother, and his mother's sister, Mary the wife of Clopas, and Mary Magdalene. When Jesus saw his mother and the disciple whom he loved standing beside her, he said to his mother, 'Woman, here is your son'. Then he said to the disciple, 'Here is your mother.' And from that hour the disciple took her into his own home.

JOHN 19:25–27

As in other places in the Gospels, we find some interesting variations between John's presentation of the events surrounding the crucifixion of Jesus and those of the other evangelists. One of these is the part played by the women. In Mark's Gospel, for instance, the women remain some distance away from the cross (15:40–41) and Matthew records that, following the arrest of Jesus, all the disciples deserted Jesus and ran away (26:56). Remarkably, after the prominence given to Mary at the beginning of Luke's Gospel, he does not mention her at all with regard to the cross.

Over the years there have been many debates concerning whether Mary was actually present at the crucifixion or not and whether the precise details of any one of the Gospel writers were in fact more accurate than the others; I don't intend to revisit those debates. Two writers who provide good summaries of these issues (despite being slightly dated) are John McHugh (*The Mother of Jesus in the New Testament*, DLT, 1975) and Max Thurian (*Mary: Mother of the Lord, Figure of the Church*, Faith Press, 1963). Whether Mary was physically present at the cross or not makes no difference for me, because I feel the very fact that John mentions it at all is hugely significant in our assessment of the wider role and function of Mary in the Church.

In John's account of the events surrounding the cross, his focus is primarily on Jesus in relation to those closest to him. I have often wondered about the link between, on the one hand, Mary's being placed under the care of Jesus' dearest disciple, and, on the other hand, the reassembling of the disciples once more in Jerusalem along with Mary, some other women and the brothers of Jesus (Acts1:14). What occurs to me is that John's unfolding of the events at the foot of the cross suggests that, when Jesus entrusted Mary to the beloved disciple and vice versa, we are being pointed to the idea that Jesus' earthly mission is completed and provision is now made for those closest to him.

But it's not sentimental

On more than one occasion in previous chapters I have made the point that Mary is far more than a faithful mother to a gentle Jesus. There is a danger of over-sentimentalising Mary as a mother and Jesus as a human son. Jesus was primarily concerned with justice for all, even at the cost of blood ties, and in some significant ways the Gospels can in fact be read as portraying a family-unfriendly Jesus. We have already seen in Chapter 2 how, in Mark's Gospel, Jesus is told that his mother and brothers and sister are outside the house asking for him (while he himself is inside). In his response, Jesus suggests that he is already in the presence of his 'real' family—those who are inside the house and not his blood family (Mark 3:34–35). This is far from the approach of many traditional picture Bibles that portray Jesus as embracing his mother and close family.

Similarly, Luke's Gospel is quite hard on blood ties. In Luke, Jesus much prefers to think of family in terms of discipleship, and he utters one of the hardest of all the New Testament sayings on the issue: 'Whoever comes to me and does not hate father and mother, wife and children, brothers and sisters, yes, and even life itself, cannot be my disciple' (Luke 14:26). Again, a picture Bible depicting a 'normal' Jesus carrying children in his arms and promoting a kind of imaginary Victorian family lifestyle would find this a difficult image to portray!

However, none of this detracts from what Jesus said to Mary and the beloved disciple as he hung on the cross. Indeed, it offers a new and radical way of understanding that event properly. It was not a conversation between what we would call an ordinary mother, son and close friend. In this situation Mary cannot be seen as a 'normal' mother (she is much more than that), so that contemporary human categories and definitions prove inadequate to describe fully the relationship between Jesus and his mother. In the final encounter she had with her son before he died on the cross, Mary emerges as the first-born of the new creation whose original 'yes' made way for the salvation of all. As we have seen, that 'yes' needed to be heard even before God could initiate the primary act of incarnation.

The hour of exaltation

In Chapter 5 I referred to Jesus saying to his mother at the wedding in Cana that his 'hour' had not yet come (John 2:4), that is, the time for recognising fully the glory of God in Jesus' mission had not yet arrived. That hour did come on the cross—it was the hour in which the love of Christ as Saviour was fully manifested. The precise nature of this hour has a deep theological significance for John. According to Paul and to the writers of the other three Gospels the hour of the cross was the hour of humiliation. For John it is rather the hour of exaltation, despite it also being the hour of Jesus' most painful suffering. In this regard it seems to me indeed important that John does not emphasise Jesus' suffering—the word 'suffering' is not even used by him. For John the cross is the hour of Jesus' greatest triumph and the ultimate manifestation of God's love for all creation and not just for those close to him (John 13:1).

This is further borne out by the very last words that the earthly Jesus utters. According to John, Jesus says 'It is finished' (19:30) and in Matthew and Mark, Jesus is said to have cried out 'My God, my God, why have you forsaken me?' (Matthew 27:46; Mark 15:34). In John we hear a cry of victory—all is accomplished and fulfilled. Alongside this, it is conceivable that John is less concerned to portray Mary as a mournful mother rather than as a witnessing disciple, sharing in the triumphant exaltation of her son. So if she did witness a triumph rather than a humiliation on that Friday afternoon outside Jerusalem, we can begin to understand how John is able to depict Mary at the foot of the cross as both a prototype and exemplar of faith, remaining with her son right to the end of his earthly life. It is precisely because of this faith that Jesus presents her to John, his most beloved disciple, as a mother in faith—here John stands as a representative of all those for whom Jesus died and whom he continues to love.

This would not be the first occasion in John's Gospel where an individual is used in a representational role. Examples would include Nicodemus, who represents learned people seeking after truth (3:1–15), and the Samaritan woman, who represents the not-so-learned people searching for the water of life (4:1–42). In this way the beloved disciple can be understood as representing all who love Jesus as well as all whom Jesus himself loves. Such love had already been promised (14:21, 23) and Jesus had already referred to 'his friends' (15:13–17) and said that, as his friends, great things would happen to them.

In this sense, I am comfortable with the use of the title 'Mother of the Church' attributed to Mary by many Christians—as 'mother' of all Jesus' friends she is closely connected to the eternal mission of Jesus. Could it be that this is truly the moment that should be regarded as the 'birthday' of the Church? As I mentioned earlier in the book, over the generations there have been countless conversations and debates as to when exactly the Church was born. Was it in the Bethlehem manger or around the table in the upper room or in the blood and water of the cross or at the discovery of the empty tomb or as the Holy Spirit descended at Pentecost? I think it may be possible to argue that the birthday of the Church may well have occurred in the encounter between Jesus, Mary and John at the foot of the cross. Jesus commands the beloved disciple not to regard Mary as Jesus' mother, but rather to recognise that Mary is 'your mother' (19:27) and as such the mother of all those people for whom John stands.

Here Mary becomes, for all people, the firstborn of a new reality, a new family that only God could create.

Mary's presence at this decisive moment shows that, along with the messianic community (represented by the beloved disciple and the other women), she shared in a profound way in the very last mystery of Jesus' eternal mission. Jesus' words to Mary and John constitute that supreme moment in the remarkable events surrounding the cross. Very soon afterwards the 'hour' is mentioned once more as not only having arrived but as having been fulfilled (19:30). The words of Jesus to Mary and John are thus placed at the very summit and accomplishment of the redemption achieved that day on the cross.

Her original 'yes' led Mary to the cross

Just as we could argue that the cross was more exaltation than humiliation, so too the annunciation was more pain than joy. By saying 'yes' to the angel, Mary inevitably allowed herself to be led to the cross. There is another significant paradox here, as much is asked of Mary—she witnesses the death of her son and, as the 'mother' of all Jesus' followers, she even becomes the mother of those who were responsible for his death.

I see resonances here with Dante's description of Mary in his *Divine Comedy*, where he uses the phrase, 'Virgin Mother, daughter of thy son'. This is a description that takes us right back to the incarnation where the annunciation to Mary becomes a model for all people who, in any way, willingly say 'yes' to God—whatever the calling. Her saying 'yes' enabled God to initiate his will of incarnation and, by bearing the incarnation, Mary journeyed with it consistently and faithfully towards the cross and beyond it into redemption. As A.M. Allchin said, 'In the annunciation made to Mary, and in her obedient and willing reply, all the mystery of human liberation from frustration and death is foreshadowed and contained' (*The Joy of All Creation*, DLT, 1984).

The famous memorial prayer to the incarnation, commonly known as the 'Dominus Angelus' (Angel of the Lord), captures the truth of this rather beautifully. It is a prayer that falls into three parts: first a recollection of the annunciation, then Mary's 'yes' and finally the incarnation. Between each of the three parts comes the prayer known as the 'Hail Mary' and it all ends with a closing prayer that connects the beginning and ending of Jesus' earthly ministry: 'We beseech you, O Lord, to pour your grace into our hearts; that as we have known the incarnation of your Son Jesus Christ by the message of an angel, so by his cross and passion we may be brought to the glory of his resurrection; through Jesus Christ our Lord. Amen.'

This prayer seeks to bring together in a most intimate and spiritually profound way, on the one hand, Bethlehem and Jerusalem, and, on the other hand, our own births and deaths—our personal experiences of Bethlehem and Jerusalem. Again, that moment of the annunciation to Mary becomes a defining moment and it provides us with a way of making sense of what we mean when we say that heaven and earth are close. Bethlehem and Jerusalem—the manger and the cross—witness, in a most remarkable way, to the liberating and transfiguring love of God that is offered to all—a love that is infinitely possible in life, but only when we are bold enough to say 'yes'.

It is in this sense that I think some of our ideas surrounding baptism are best understood. In his letter to the Romans, Paul urges us to make the link between our own baptisms and the death of Jesus Christ. He says 'Do you not know that all of us who have been baptised into Christ Jesus were baptised into his death? Therefore we have been buried with him by baptism into death, so that, just as Christ was raised from the dead by the glory of the Father, so we too might walk in newness of life' (Romans 6:3–4). Here, again, Bethlehem and Jerusalem become as one—through Bethlehem, all our births are connected to the manger so that life may be open to the liberating love of God. Through Jerusalem, all our baptisms are connected to the cross, so that ultimately all our deaths may be a dying and rising to the transfiguring power of the risen Christ. A.M. Allchin referred to the font as the 'womb of the church', being of one substance with the womb of Mary. This is yet another way of understanding Mary as the mother of all Christians.

Mary—the new Abraham

In talking about Mary as the mother of all Christians and linking her womb with the womb of the church, we could go back to link the womb of creation itself represented by Eve. As already mentioned, connections between Mary and Eve have often been made, particularly in connection with the idea of Mary as the new Eve—the obedience and 'yes' of Mary overturning the disobedience and 'no' of Eve. In the same way, connections and comparisons are often made between Jesus and other figures in the Old Testament—Jesus as the new Adam or the new Moses or the new David. He is never referred to as the new Abraham, and I sometimes wonder whether Mary is truly our new Abraham, particularly as she stands at the foot of the cross.

Abraham did not resist God's call to leave his father's country to go to a new land (Genesis 12:1–4), just as Mary did not resist God's declaration that she was to bear a child through the power of the Holy Spirit. Abraham's faith foreshadows Mary's 'yes' because, just as we are Abraham's children through faith, so we are children of the new covenant, inaugurated in Christ, through Mary's 'yes'. At the eleventh hour, God restrained Abraham from sacrificing his son Isaac (22:11–12), but God did not hold back from sacrificing Mary's son. So we could actually read Jesus' command that Mary should look on John as her son as a request: he is asking his mother to see that the one born of her body has to be sacrificed and lost to her as a son, so that we might live.

Not Jesus' mother but 'your mother'

In his meditations on the seven last words uttered by Christ on the cross, the American theologian Stanley Hauerwas states that Jesus' words 'behold your son' to Mary were actually a request for her to witness the sacrifice taking place on the cross (*Cross-Shattered Christ*, DLT, 2006). Without saying a word, Mary stood and watched her son enter the darkness of the cross, holding fast to the promises she had received long ago in Nazareth. It was a promise that the son whom she now watched dying would eventually scatter the proud, bring down the powerful from their thrones, fill the hungry with good things and fulfil the promises made to Abraham and his descendants; all of this would be ultimately accomplished on the cross.

The request that Mary should regard John as her own family is an invitation to an act of discipleship. At the foot of the cross all people of all generations are invited to enter the mystery of God's redeeming love as the Church is born at that moment. In his meditation on the words of Jesus from the cross, Hauerwas makes the interesting point that the Church (and by that he means the people, not the building) contains Mary's home—a home, he says, that promises not safety but rather the ongoing challenge of being a people called from the nations to be God's people, or, as I sometimes like to put it, a people of the annunciation. This is a new family of people, united by faith in the one who hung on that cross, refusing to triumph by the ways of the world—a world that believed and, tragically, continues to believe, that violence is eminently justifiable.

End the dispersion of God's people

From the cross, Jesus addresses his mother with the word 'woman', a word he had used to address others on several previous occasions—the Samaritan woman (John 4:21), the woman taken in adultery (8:10) and Mary Magdalene (20:15). The context of each of these previous occasions is interesting as they are all times when Jesus stands in solidarity with vulnerability, with the aim of avoiding any potential injustice. These times are thus contexts of liberation. In using the word 'woman' to address his mother from the cross, he is purposely bringing liberation into the lives of those gathered at the cross and beyond—the new community of God's people. And these people are no longer the *anawim* but a new transfigured people.

In their assessment of these events surrounding the cross, Ivone Gebara and Maria Clara Bingemer remind us that the early church understood the death of Jesus as a means of gathering God's dispersed people (11:51–52). They point out that in the Old Testament tradition there is a clear thread of attempts to disperse God's people and wipe out their identity and traditions, thus making them a non-people—*anawim*. Usually these dispersed people are identified as the marginalised, victims of oppression and the persecuted, who, by the time of the New Testament, are reunited through the proclamation of an inclusive kingdom which was ushered into the world through the life of Jesus.

One of the responsibilities of the Old Testament prophets—seen most clearly in the events of the exile—was to keep these dispersed people together and bring them back to the security and blessing of Jerusalem. In the spirit of the prophets who accompanied the exiles back to Jerusalem and proclaimed a reuniting of God's dispersed people (Ezra 1:1–4), a dying Jesus says from the cross to his mother, 'Woman, here is your son' (John 19:26). Gebara and Bingemer recognise here a figure of the Israel that gives birth to the new people, of the Jerusalem that brings the dispersed—the *anawim*—back together in the temple. They see God giving birth to the Christian community, the people of the new covenant symbolised in Mary and the beloved disciple, who stand at the foot of the cross, representing everyone who follows Jesus. So the Gospel of John—pre-eminently the Gospel of the passion—places Mary at the very centre of the ultimate event of redemption and holds her as a symbol of the people who will accept the power of the kingdom and the fullness of the messianic age.

However, despite the cross being a moment of glorious exaltation, a possible birthday for the Church and a place where Mary becomes a universal mother, it must also be seen as a place of real and deep anguish.

Power among the ruins

Ever since I was a child I have been fascinated by ruins and I often remember how I enjoyed playing with friends for hours in a ruined quarrying village—imagining the destruction, pondering the history, thinking about who lived where and dreaming of its reconstruction. The fascination runs deeper, though, and endures through my experiences as one interested in pilgrimage. As a pilgrim I often end up in places looking at ruined churches or ruined monuments, and using them as metaphors to encourage an exploration of our own sense of ruin in life as well as the potential of seeing light shining out through the cracks of those personal ruins.

A ruin is much more than a dilapidated building or a monument lying on its back. It can also be a state of mind or a fragmented life situation, as it was for the exiles of the Old Testament. The Jewish people bewailed their ruined lives as they struggled to come to terms with an exile far away from their ruined temple, but the prophets still encouraged them to search for a light that could shine through the cracks of their ruins. For them, that light was the hope of returning to Jerusalem.

So much of the Old Testament dream centres on the hope of returning home and living once again in a redeemed and restored Israel, in very physical terms. For the exiles, the establishing of a new age was not a far-fetched utopia in which everything leading to their estrangement and exile could be cancelled and forgotten. The prophets firmly believed that in order to begin again they needed to return to the ruins of the past—the devastated and destroyed city (Isaiah 61:4). This meant going back to face old painful memories and redeeming them.

Pictures of ruins also interest me—and one picture in particular has stayed with me for a long time. It comes from the closing shot of the 1983 film *Nostalgia*, directed by Andrey Tarkovsky, and has been used as the cover illustration for Philip Sheldrake's book *Spaces for the Sacred; Place, Memory and Identity* (SCM Press, 2001). The picture shows a small house built within the ruins of an old abbey with light shining through the remains of that ruined abbey's window spaces. The picture speaks to me of the possibilities and opportunities that lie deep within the image and metaphor of ruin—of finding home even among the ruins of a glory that has once been. Rowan Williams imagines this in terms of a process by which ruins can truly become places to live in and asks the sobering question, 'What would it be like to see ruins as home? What might it be to see them now as a potential home?' ('Love among the ruins', *Church Times*, 24 December 1998).

In his book *After Virtue* (Duckworth, 1982) Alasdair Macintyre makes an interesting and slightly different use of this idea of ruin. He asks his readers to imagine that the history of human existence falls into three particular epochs. First, there was a time when everything was rosy, and people knew and understood each other, sharing several commonalities—language, traditions and culture, for instance. The second epoch was a time of great change; a time when those shared values were thrown into an imaginary fire so as to make way for a new start. The third was a time of deep regret when the people wished they had never even lit that fire; they now searched for ways to salvage what had once kept them together. However, it was too late and they were only able to rescue from the embers of that fire bits of traditions, pages of books and snippets of the old ways. All had become ruins in this third epoch but the process of making sense of these ruins was only possible by working together and not alone—that was the challenge.

Macintyre's book suggests that we can think about this image of ruin in theological terms. Indeed, the very reason for God wishing an incarnation in the first place was to bring love into a ruined world—ruin was the original context for incarnation and as Jesus approached the cross, a sense of ruin was very much in the air. Indeed, much about the passion of Christ and the events leading up to the cross was ruin in a very deep sense. This was certainly true for the disciples. Their world was falling apart and, disappointingly for them, a crown of thorns replaced their dream of a crown of glory. Both Jesus' birth and his death are set within a context of a landscape of loss, destruction, haunted and half-forgotten ruined stones.

Gazing into the eyes of her dying son must have made Mary wonder how she was going to see this ruin of the cross in hopeful ways. How was all of this part of the promise of incarnation? How was humiliation going to be turned into exaltation here on the cross? We will never know for certain what she thought or even glimpsed that day, but, by pondering the power of the words that were shared at the foot of the cross, in the light of the rest of the story, we begin to explore the new world defined by Christ. What did Mary make of all this? We will only begin to find out by letting the difficult words and images of ruin come to life for us.

Another stone but no ruin

There is another 'stone' that helps us see that humiliation did become exaltation for Mary, but this stone is certainly not a ruin. As a millennium treat I went to Rome for the first time. It was an extraordinary experience in different ways and I shall never forget my first encounter with the spiritual and cultural richness of St Peter's Basilica. I spent time exploring almost every corner of that international place of pilgrimage and what has remained with me above all is Michelangelo's *Pietà*.

Michelangelo was only 23 years old when he was commissioned to produce this sculpture in 1498 but to my mind he managed to produce one of the most astonishing representations of Mary. The sculpture shows Jesus lifeless on his mother's lap after his deposition from the cross, and it is intended to evoke 'compassion' (*pietà*) in those who view it. Unlike so many other depictions of the mourning Mary—anguished and wailing—this one shows beauty and acceptance. Michelangelo shows us a Mary without a furrow or a wrinkle—a visible representation of Paul's description of the Church of which Mary is a figure, presented 'in splendour, without a spot or wrinkle or anything of the kind' (Ephesians 5:27).

I get the impression that Michelangelo envisions Mary's 'yes' as more than just passive acceptance; it is also active cooperation in the wider story of God's redeeming mission. Mary tenderly cradles the body of her son with her left hand, while the right hand has already released him and opens in a gesture of offering. This, for me, is further confirmation that at the foot of the cross Mary encountered exaltation at its greatest rather than humiliation. Michelangelo showed through this gesture of Mary's right hand a direct invitation for all people to share in that eternal moment of exaltation. What we encounter in the *Pietà* is a timeless example for men and women of the greatness that can be achieved if one can just say 'yes' to God.

Incarnation, then cross and then grace

Finally, I want to take the image of ruin just one step further: around the cross I also see a ruined people. In one sense this can actually be comforting because, generally speaking, a basic characteristic of people living among ruins is a refusal to collude with the conspiracy of success that too often characterises even a religious structure. The cross was a 'no' to all such conspiracy. Many people who live with and alongside ruin have rejected the bright and shining life of human perfectibility and have learned to live with only two certainties: their own frailty and the forgiveness of Christ. Somewhat precariously, they live by grace and they minister such grace to others, often without realising it.

For me, it is only at the end of the earthly life of Jesus that we begin truly to come to terms with the Word becoming flesh in all its uncertainty and awkwardness. Grace came to Mary at the foot of the cross as she looked at her ruin; so often, grace comes to us through weakness—and that's the paradox of grace, once again. Uncertainty, confusion and incompetence surround both the manger and the cross—Bethlehem and Jerusalem—and yet somewhere an angel sings because God has found another member of the *anawim* in which to dwell.

Part 4

Abiding voice of freedom

One of the words that kept popping up in my mind during the course of researching and writing this book was 'covenant'. I have resisted the temptation of building on the concept of covenant in previous chapters so as to be able to focus on it in this concluding section. The reason why covenant has occupied much of my thinking is because I believe that God intended his relationship with Mary to be the quintessential covenant experience, carrying with it echoes of the covenants of the Old Testament—covenants that God had already created with others. If, in the person of Jesus, God's creation enters a new and crucial phase—and this is clearly revealed at various stages in Jesus' life and ministry—then the story of Mary certainly has the power of covenant about it.

And God breathes into us the breath of life

One of the most consistent themes running right through the Old Testament is the Israelites' concern with their relationship as a nation both with God and with the world in which they lived. Although they recognised that as a people their journey began in 'dust' (Genesis 2:7) and that they were essentially mortal and vulnerable, suddenly they began to flourish when God vitalised the dust and gave it spirit (Genesis 1:3; Genesis 2:7b; Psalm 33:6). The Spirit or breath of God is the overwhelming Old Testament principle of life for all living things—people survive by the communication of God's spirit (Genesis 2:7; 6:17; 7:15; Job 33:4; Ecclesiastes 3:19, 21). Chapter 1 of Genesis explicitly states that this is a communicative process by which human beings were gifted with a godly dignity which became an integral part of the divine/human relationship (Genesis 1:26–27). The book of Genesis is also clear that this dignity was a gift given to both sexes, and the female emerged as the result of a distinct and wonderful creative act—she is the only living being fit to accompany Adam. Although she is not actually named at this point, I still believe that she is given exactly the same dignity as Adam and is in no way inferior; the same spirit was breathed into both (Genesis 2:18–25).

Here we see the basis of a unique relationship between God and humanity, in which the first step towards the relationship comes from a positive action by God, which is then reciprocated by a positive human action, and thus a covenant is formed. Although the idea of covenant is used in various ways throughout the Old Testament, it is the one made between God and humans that emerges as dominant. It runs through the books of Exodus, Leviticus, Numbers and Deuteronomy as the central experience of the unfolding drama. In these books God initiates the covenant through a process known as election, and in many 'saving acts' the elected people are given identity, stability and unity. Election is essentially based on God's love (Deuteronomy 4:37; 7:6) and is never a godly reward for greatness and merit. It is a call to responsibility and obligation, not privilege and favouritism.

While covenant occupies a central place in the writings of both the Pentateuch and the historical books (from the book of Joshua through to the books of Kings and Chronicles), it is not used directly by many of the prophets. What is interesting is how the experience of covenant is woven through the prophetic message but often without directly mentioning the word. Prophets such as Amos, Hosea, Isaiah and Micah present throughout their ministry the fundamental thrust of what it meant to be a covenanted people—living under God's sovereignty and also God's saving acts of love. However, the book of the prophet Jeremiah offers a new perspective on this covenant relationship between Israel and God. In his message to the people of the early sixth century BC, he shows that it is precisely because the covenant is both a source of obligation and a blessing that God shows faithfulness to his covenanted people even when they are punished for their violations. Jeremiah imagines the future of Israel in terms of a new covenant (31:31–34) and stresses that this will establish a personal relationship between God and individuals—not necessarily a nation. Although the earliest covenants were indeed formed with individuals, the whole nation was ultimately affected and called to respond. Jeremiah brings it all into a much more personal context and suggests that under the new covenant, it is the individual who is called to say 'yes'.

God's covenanted people

One of the earliest biblical covenants was the one God forged with Noah (Genesis 9:8–17), but this particular covenant is a relationship established between God and all the created order, not just people. The book of Genesis is clear that human beings have always been in a special relationship with the whole of God's creation and when Noah took animals into the ark, he thus exercised the proper stewardship for which people were created. Interestingly, unlike almost all other covenants, the one with Noah does not depend upon any action by the human partner. The rainbow was a sign of God's undertaking to guarantee the natural order of things—seasons, crops, food. We might say that building the ark and preserving the species was a demand placed upon Noah, but notice that the actual covenant is formed after the floods cease. It promises a new created order and all the action is on God's side, asking for nothing in return.

Then comes God's covenant with Abraham (Genesis 17) and, as with Noah, the action is almost entirely on God's side, although God does ask a little more of Abraham. In many ways Abraham emerges as the original key player in the whole of the Old Testament. He was the first of the patriarchs and as such is regarded as the founder of the Jewish nation. It is not without significance that all three of the monotheistic faiths—Jewish, Muslim and Christian—regard him as a father figure who was dignified, firm in his faith, humane and respected by local rulers. He moves slowly and majestically across the Middle Eastern world of nearly 4000 years ago, from Mesopotamia to Egypt, but the main setting for his story is the central hill country in the land of Canaan, promised to him and his ancestors by God.

Trevor Dennis, an Anglican biblical writer, claims that Abraham was the first person to look God directly in the eye (*Looking God in the Eye*, SPCK, 1998). But Abraham did not simply look God in the eye and converse honestly and openly with him, he was also the first to say 'yes' to God and this 'yes' was the basis of the covenant between him and God. Abraham's covenant is a reminder of the way in which faith is rooted in the initiative that God takes in order to establish a relationship with his people. It is then for them to respond in the way Abraham and others have done. Like the covenant with Noah, this is one in which there is no bargaining but which is based firmly on the fact that the one who promises is God. Although elsewhere Abraham is bold enough at least to try his hand at a bit of bargaining with God (Genesis 18), all he has to do in the original covenant is to recognise what God is like and trust him so that God is able to fulfil the promises he makes.

Then there is the third major covenant, but this one is quite different (Exodus 20:1–17). Part of this third covenant is the giving of the commandments to Moses on Sinai. The commandments function as a sign of a relationship with God in which again God takes the initiative, in which God guarantees the future and in which God sets out the conditions on which the covenant relationship is dependent. The commandments are offered as a sign that God rejoices in the fact that a covenant has been created between him and his people, but now a certain way of life is required of them to keep their part of the relationship alive and healthy. They are called to root their relationships both with God and with one another in the faith; this new covenant gave them serious work to do.

A covenant now promises the Messiah

All the covenants mentioned so far have a lasting prominence because of their place in the Torah—the heart of the whole Jewish religious structure. But the second book of Samuel (7:11–16; see also Psalm 89:19–37) sets out yet another crucial covenant, this time between God and David, and it is one that cannot be ignored from a Christian perspective. Significantly, this is the covenant referred to by Isaiah (55:3) in a section of his book designed as a glorious finale to what is commonly called Isaiah's Book of Comfort (chapters 40—55), where almost all the themes are blended together. Throughout chapter 55 Isaiah retraces previous themes and connects them closely to the covenant with David. Such themes include a new exodus (Isaiah 40:1–11; 55:12–13) the way of the Lord (40:3, 27; 55:7–9) the call to pasture (40:11; 55:1–2), the word of the Lord (40:8; 55:11), kingship (40:10, 23; 55:3–5), heaven and earth (40:12; 55:8–11), Israel (40:12–31; 55:6–11), forgiveness (40:2; 55:7) and the participation of the nations (40:4; 55:12). The covenant with David is called an *everlasting covenant* (55:3)—it does not begin now and last forever, but brings the promises and prophecies of the past to a present fulfilment in the figure of the Messiah (Isaiah 24:5; 59:21; 61:8; Ezekiel 37:26–28; Matthew 26:28; Luke 22:20).

Throughout Isaiah's Book of Comfort we discover several divine paradoxes. God is transcendent and hidden (45:15), yet near enough to be concerned with human frailty (43:24). Men and women are referred to as God's children (43:1–7), yet they are also called to act as adults. Interestingly, 55:10–11 speaks in terms of a God promising to send his *word* to his people not as something suspended in the air like clouds but rather more like an energy that will soak the earth. It is a covenant that speaks of God's spirit infusing itself in the lives of people in which divine fruits will be yielded. All of this is not simply a message from God—that is not what covenants are—but rather an event that is promised (41:17–20); a real event perceived in the mystery of God's saving acts (44:24—45:8).

Isaiah is keen to end his Book of Comfort by recalling the Exodus theme and connecting it to the experience of covenant—all the world, he says, will break out into song as God brings his children back wondrously. This re-establishment of God's reign constitutes *an everlasting sign* (55:13) of divine love, and ultimately the entire world will come to recognise God as Saviour. The American Old Testament scholar Walter Brueggemann in his commentary on the book of Isaiah senses in chapter 55 an almost cosmic significance to these verses (*Isaiah 40—66, Westminster Bible Companion,* Westminster John Knox Press, 1998). Although written in the context of liberation from Babylonian exile, the promise is bigger. He says that 'thorn and brier' (55:13) are words commonly used by Isaiah to refer to a diminished life generally (5:6; 7:23–25; 27:4; 32:13). In the coming of the new age these negative prickly plants are overcome and pronounced null and void. These prickles of nullity will be replaced by new vibrant signs of growth, life and beauty—the 'cypress and myrtle' (55:13). Brueggemann rightly suggests that the homecoming of Israel symbolises the eventual promise of the healing of all creation. It speaks passionately of the promised signs and witnesses of God's new transfiguring and liberating kingdom. Isaiah's interpretation of covenant has about it a deep resonance of the promise of incarnation and of the coming of a saviour.

A new covenant of incarnation

In the New Testament, although the Gospels do not spell out the concept in quite the same way as the Old Testament, the whole of the Gospel narrative can be read as one big covenant. All four evangelists, in different ways, set the story of Jesus as a dramatic conflict between Jesus the Son of God, the light that has come into the world (incarnation), and the powers of darkness already prevalent in the world (cross). If, as I mentioned earlier, in the person of Jesus God's creation has entered a new and crucial phase, then clearly the whole of the Gospels is a covenant par excellence that, as with the Mosaic one, has fundamental implications for those who respond in discipleship. The New Testament covenant is one that demands of us a response as to how we form, develop and nurture our relationship with each other and with God.

So God now enters into a very special covenant with Mary—a covenant of incarnation by which God enters the world in transfiguring and liberating power. This covenant with Mary is also intrinsically linked to the actual in-breaking of the kingdom of God through the life, ministry, death and resurrection of Jesus. It is also a covenant that—like the New Testament covenant as a whole—carries heavy implications for those who profess the faith of the risen Christ. It is precisely these implications that I now want to explore and I will focus on Mary's continuing ministry, firstly as a witness to God's abiding and transfiguring power, and secondly as a continuing challenge to us to respond positively to Christ's prayer that his people should be united, should be as one.

However, my guiding principle in these final two chapters will be the way in which all Christians are challenged by the coming of the kingdom of God in and through the incarnation of Jesus and the way in which every Christian is invited into a covenant relationship with God. In Chapter 7 I will concentrate on the way in which the story of Mary has a continuing ministry in the life of the modern church. Some Christians express this ministry by visiting specific places associated with Mary and claim that those places continue to witness God's transfiguring power today. Whether we belong to such spiritual traditions or not, most Christians accept that there is something about these places that is profoundly compelling. They symbolise aspects of Mary's life that offer hope to people who struggle—whether with issues relating to health, status, gender or indeed faith.

Then in Chapter 8 I want to end by revisiting Christ's final address to his disciples in the upper room (John 13:31—17:36). In it Jesus prays that his followers (then as today) will be one people united in the faith. Sadly, the truth is different and on the whole Christians are so often divided. Sadly, Mary, too, has often in history been regarded as a figure of division and contention. I want to end with a rallying call that this is a tragedy and should not be the case—that instead of being a reason for division Mary can in fact be a real focus of unity.

Kingdom united

However, my closing call will also have a note of urgency about it—an urgency that is found in that Jesus' speech in John as well. Whether we come from a part of the Church familiar with Marian customs and devotions or not, one thing is certain: as contemporary disciples of Jesus Christ there are certain matters that must remain beyond dispute, non-optional and obligatory for us all. These are the implications of the covenant with God that all Christians are invited to enter into—just like Noah, Abraham, Moses and Mary:

- Christians today—whatever their church tradition—are called by God to say 'yes' when invited to proclaim with joy the good news of the kingdom of God.
- Christians today—whatever their church tradition—are called by God to say 'yes' when invited to respond lovingly to the needs of people, whoever and whatever they are.
- Christians today—whatever their church tradition—are called by God to say 'yes' when invited to do all they possibly can to transform all that is unjust and unfair in society.
- Christians today—whatever their church tradition—are called by God to say 'yes' when invited to defend the natural world created by God and to play their part in the process of transfiguring the life of this world.

Chapter 7

Witnessing God's transfiguring power

And Mary said, 'My soul magnifies the Lord, and my spirit rejoices in God my Saviour, for he has looked with favour on the lowliness of his servant. Surely, from now on all generations will call me blessed; for the Mighty One has done great things for me, and holy is his name. His mercy is for those who fear him from generation to generation.'
LUKE 1:46–50

Mary's song of praise, in which she extols God for all that he is doing for the human race through her son, must be the most popular biblical passage with which most Christians associate Mary. Its main focus is that of rejoicing in God's fulfilment of an age-old promise and, as the actual bearer of God's incarnation, Mary will be honoured by all God's people in the new age of salvation begun through the incarnation. This song of praise follows a similar pattern to three other songs associated with the birth of Jesus in Luke's Gospel—Zechariah's prophecy at the birth of John the Baptist (1:67–79), angels praising God at the birth of Jesus (2:13–14) and Simeon's song of thanksgiving at the presentation of Jesus in the temple (vv. 28–32).

Mary's song of praise also shows significant parallels with similar songs in the Old Testament, such as the song of Hannah (1 Samuel 2:1–10) in which Hannah rejoices at the birth of her unexpected son Samuel and presents him to God as a thank-offering. In much the same way, Mary's song resembles the so-called 'hymns of praise' that appear in the Psalms (33, 47, 48, 113, 117, 135, 136) where, like Mary, the singers praise God for all that he has achieved and given to his people. These 'hymns of praise' in the Psalms, just like the first part of Mary's song, sing of three particular divine attributes: God's might, God's holiness and God's mercy.

Like Hannah, who sings of God's greatness and recognises God as her saviour, Mary rejoices in the covenant that God has formed with her. Mary acknowledges that through this covenant a new opportunity for salvation is offered to people—not just to Mary—through the birth of her son. Mary's mention of her own humility in all that is happening to her further highlights God's might, God's holiness and God's mercy. She seems quite certain that all that is happening to her will be remembered forever, not because, it seems to me, of any intrinsic personal holiness or merit, but because of him whom she is bearing.

Mary's continuing ministry

In the introduction to Part 4 I mentioned the way in which God now enters into a very special covenant with Mary—a covenant of incarnation by which God enters the world in transfiguring and liberating power. Intrinsic to this covenant of incarnation are those three divine attributes of old which reveal themselves again—God's might, God's holiness and God's mercy. It was not a covenant for covenant's sake, nor was it an incarnation for incarnation's sake—God was on a mission and he had work to do.

My intention in citing only the first part of Mary's song

(Luke 1:46–50) at the start of this chapter is to underline what I feel is a significant aspect of the song. All too often—and especially in a liberation context—the focus of this song hinges on those later verses that sing of God's power in scattering the proud, bringing down the powerful and sending the rich away empty (vv. 51–53). Of course, these are crucial statements, but they sometimes cast a shadow over the opening words of the song that mention those people, who, from generation to generation (forever), will remember Mary and praise her as the bearer of the incarnation. In this chapter I want to unpack what it means to 'remember' Mary for ever and whether that memorial carries with it the implication that Mary has a 'continuing ministry' witnessing to God's abiding and transfiguring power.

There are three areas in which Christians of every tradition can speak with confidence of Mary as having a continuing ministry. The first is concerned with the role she continues to play in what is commonly called popular or folk religion. The second brings us right back to the idea of *anawim* and the sense in which all our 'Christian seeds' can be traced back to Mary and her role in God's initiation of a new age. If that initiatory role is in fact real then Mary, implicitly so, has an ongoing ministry because the vibrancy of that new age continues today. The third takes us to physical and specific places. At the heart of the Christian tradition, the idea of pilgrimage, as both action and metaphor, continues to fascinate people, and many of those places celebrate Mary both as mother of Jesus and a woman with a continuing concern for a troubled world for which she watched her son dying.

Mary at the heart of popular devotion

The relationship between traditional Christian belief and popular devotion is a very ancient one. Indeed, the way in which Christians of all backgrounds have sought to interpret the fundamentals of the faith and integrate them into their own spiritual lives has had a profound influence on the history of the Church and of society in general. Realistically, it is impossible to make sense of the history of spirituality and the Church without paying serious attention to the way in which local communities across the world have grappled with the great dogmas of faith and made them accessible to their own needs.

In his book *Mary Through the Centuries* (Yale University Press, 1996) Jaroslav Pelikan makes the simple but crucial point that a major component in the formation of traditional Christian teaching has been liturgy, creed and dogma. However, he raises a question as to whether the historians and theologians of later ages should assume that what the councils of the Church legislated as liturgy, creed and dogma was in fact what the common people believed and practised. Is it not more the case that what the people believe and practise is actually different from the traditional liturgy, creed and dogma? In fact, the real meaning of popular religion is probably to be sought in the categories of race, class and gender and the ways in which these impact upon religious traditions. Pelikan believes that it is important for the Church to be open at least to exploring the impact of people's experiences of race, class and gender on liturgy, creed and dogma rather than the other way round.

In truth, this is nothing new. Both the New Testament period and subsequent years in the development of the early

Church are marked by a fusion of popular religious practices that later became liturgy, creed and dogma. From the earliest Christian communities, Christ alone (Colossians 2:17) was most important in popular religious practice, together with his life-giving word (John 6:63), his commandment of reciprocal love (13:34) and the ritual actions which he commanded in his memory (1 Corinthians 11:24–26). Everything else—days and months, seasons and years, feasts, new moons, food and drink (Galatians 4:8–11; Colossians 2:16–19)—was of secondary importance.

The signs of the local—popular devotions and piety—are already to be found among the first generation of Christians. Inspired by the Jewish tradition, they recommended following the example of incessant prayer of Jesus (Luke 18:1) and Paul (Romans 12:12; 1 Thessalonians 5:17) and of beginning and ending all activities with an act of thanksgiving (1 Corinthians 10:31; 1 Thessalonians 2:13; Colossians 3:17). Pious Jews began the day praising and giving thanks to God and, in the same spirit, gave thanks for all their activities during the course of the day. Hence every joyful or sorrowful occasion gave rise to particular local expressions. The Gospels and other New Testament writings contain invocations of Jesus, signs of Christological devotion, which were repeated spontaneously outside the context of liturgy, creed and dogma. An example of this is Jesus' saying that the sabbath was made for people and not the other way around (Mark 2:27) which is still used today in secular contexts to stress priorities. Throughout this early period, liturgy, creed and dogma, on the one hand, and popular piety and devotion, on the other hand, did not either conceptually or pastorally oppose each other.

From ancient Judah to modern-day Poland

Issues of liturgy, creed and dogma surrounding the person of Mary raise some very interesting questions. It occurs to me that a celebration of Mary's life—in whatever guise—still has an influence and impact on many parts of the modern world. This is significantly so in contexts of persecution and anti-religious propaganda and was particularly the case during the Communist era in Eastern and Central Europe. In quite astonishing ways, during those turbulent times, Mary seemed to provide an impetus by which modern-day prophets were able to encourage Christians to move from a deep sense of exile and injustice to a place of liberation and faith—just like the earlier prophets in the biblical tradition.

During King Uzziah's reign, for instance, the kingdom of Judah reached the peak of its strength. Under Ahaz (Uzziah's grandson) the situation deteriorated rapidly but, although Ahaz was a weak leader, he was supported by the prophet Isaiah. The king needed to make a decision regarding the future prosperity of Judah and some of his advisors said one thing and Isaiah another. Ahaz sought confirmation of Isaiah's words but despite the sign spoken of, 'Therefore the Lord himself will give you a sign. Look, the young woman is with child and shall bear a son, and shall name him Immanuel' (Isaiah 7:14), his mind was already closed. Although Isaiah could not persuade the king, sometime in the future the sign would confirm the truth of what he had spoken. The child promised would guarantee the kingdom's future and for this reason he could be called Immanuel because the eventual fulfilment of Isaiah's promise would reveal the closeness and intimacy of God.

Not far from my home is a large Polish community

and over the years I have befriended many Polish priests and accompanied them to almost every corner of Poland, including Częstochowa, which is linked to one of the most charming of the legends concerning Mary. It tells how, in fulfilment of Jesus' dying words, she went to live with John, the beloved disciple, in Ephesus, taking with her a table that Jesus had made, on which Luke painted a portrait of Mary. Eventually the portrait reached Poland and was hung in the monastery of Jasna Góra (the 'Luminous Mountain') in Częstochowa, where it remains to this day, known as the Black Madonna of Jasna Góra.

Over the years Poland has suffered greatly and this pilgrimage site has been the focus of continuous prayer in the face of persecution. Just as in the days of Isaiah and Ahaz, Poland has been faced with significant decisions. Unlike Ahaz, the Polish nation—especially the thousands of its young people who continue to gather daily at the shrine of Mary in Częstochowa to pray—has remained committed to God. On one of his visits to Częstochowa, Pope John Paul II said 'to be a Christian is to be on a constant vigil. As a mother is on vigil by her child, to be on a vigil is to protect the value of good.'

Popular devotion to Mary, then, is an important phenomenon running right through the life of the Church. Its expressions are multifarious and its motivation profound, deriving as it does from deep within people's faith in Jesus Christ, as redeemer, and from an awareness of the continuing ministry that God entrusted to Mary. This awareness of Mary's mission is to be seen in the way people generally understand the vital link uniting mother and son. They realise that the Son is God and that Mary, the mother, is also in a unique way their own mother. In so many religious traditions in the world the poor feel especially close to Mary and know that she, like them, was at one time poor and suffered greatly. They can identify with her suffering at the crucifixion and death of her son, as well as rejoice with her in his resurrection.

Mary and the mystics

In their attempts to renew their own relationship with Christ, many of the Christian mystics and spiritual writers have turned to Mary, and they continue to do so, often through prayers and poems. The Christian mystical tradition grew out of a sense of needing to seek ways to journey from all that is visible and tangible on earth and discover a deeper spiritual place much closer to heaven. Mary's role in such journeying is not sentimental but rather transforming—many mystics claim that by experiencing Mary, they become more empowered to experience life as God wills them to experience it.

One of the most well-known and still influential Christian mystics is Julian of Norwich (1342–1416). According to her own writings, on 8 May 1373, while seriously ill, she received a series of 15 revelations in a state of ecstatic prayer, which lasted five hours, with a further revelation on the following day. Approximately 25 years later Julian wrote about her experiences in her book *Revelations of Divine Love*. One of the hallmarks of her writings is the way she explores in wonderfully creative ways some profound aspects of theology and spirituality—the crucifixion of Christ, God as Creator, humanity and love, God as mother and the Trinity. For Julian, Mary is a major role model, not merely as a historical figure but as someone to whom she relates in her own day. Julian says: 'In this I was taught that every contemplative soul to whom it was given to look and to seek will see Mary and pass on to God through contemplation' (Julian of Norwich, *Revelations of Divine Love*, Penguin, 1966). Her point is that by saying 'yes' to God, Mary continuously offers Christians a pattern for finding ways of seeking God and deepening one's spiritual perception.

It was in my reading of chapter 4 of Julian of Norwich's *Revelations of Divine Love* that I became aware of how it is possible to talk in terms of 'annunciation moments' in all of our lives—something I mentioned in Chapter 5. What is striking about her *Revelations* is that Julian felt she had to cultivate an attitude of receptivity before she could receive the visions. It is in this way that Mary and her experiences in Nazareth became a model for Julian—she suggests that Mary's attitude of receptivity should be at the root of our personal covenants with God.

Two further aspects of Julian of Norwich's writings are, I think, relevant to our thinking on Mary, albeit indirectly. First, she refers in particular to the 'motherhood of God in Christ'. In his book *The English Mystics* (SPCK, 1998) the Anglican priest Tarjei Park suggests that there has been a tendency to see Julian as a kind of 'proto-eco-feminist'. While admitting that there are clear signs of liberation theology in her writings, he points out that Julian was at the same time a woman of her age. She lived in difficult times—plague, war, religious persecutions. In much the same way, Mary was a 'woman of her age'—an age of crisis and turmoil but also one saturated with religious fervour, and in it she bore the Messiah.

The second aspect is Julian's reference to the importance of the unity of 'substance' and 'sensuality' in the human soul.

Tarjei Park sees here a movement away from a tradition that regarded personal sensuality as an aspect of one's humanity that lay outside the rational soul and was therefore, by implication, unspiritual. For Julian, sensuality is very much part of personal spiritual substance, precisely because of the union achieved by Christ in the incarnation through Mary. In the incarnation, Christ united himself to our common humanity when he took flesh in Mary's womb and raised our humanity to a spiritual level (potentially at least) by uniting our sensuality—our body of flesh and blood with its senses and emotions—to our substance, the essential humanity of each of us as this exists in the mind of God.

Here Julian reveals a depth of wholeness in the way she so readily tackles controversial issues, especially when we bear in mind that she was writing in the 14th century. For her, all aspects of human life were intertwined and spiritual. A human being's spiritual union with God only happens because God is the Creator; the human ability to perceive God arises from deep within the individual soul primarily because men and women were created with a capacity for God.

Beyond gender

I have already dealt in some detail with several of the issues surrounding the femininity of Mary and the importance of seeking a balanced gender approach in our theological reflection (see Chapter 3). In this present discussion about Mary's continuing ministry I would like to add one further thought. The key word for me has always been 'balance' and I have a hunch that, while people have been drawn to Mary's humble 'yes', they have also been drawn to her defiance and victory (Luke 1:51–53). I suspect her talk of putting down the mighty, filling the hungry with good things and sending the rich away with nothing have encouraged a deeper exploration of what it means to be a woman. Jaroslav Pelikan claims that because Mary is *the* woman par excellence, the subtleties and complexities involved in interpreting her person and her role are central to the place of women in history, which has begun to claim its proper share both of scholarly and of popular attention.

As far as Mary's continuing ministry is concerned I think we can go—indeed, must go—one step beyond gender balance and speak more in terms of gender transcendence. It is one thing to seek balance, as opposed to an imbalance on the one hand and absolute equality on the other hand; it is one step further to seek a transcendence of gender. Mary has an important role in symbolising those divine qualities of a God who is beyond all gender. It can be argued that Judaism and Christianity have traditionally used somewhat entrenched patriarchal images and language to portray God, but in reality they also depict him as being beyond models of male and female. I think one example of this is the biblical image of Spirit. We recognise the obvious maleness of Jesus and the obvious femininity of Mary, but no such obviousness exists when it comes to God encountering the world through his Spirit. As God's Spirit hovers over the waters at creation (Genesis 1:2), images of male and female are transcended. Similarly, when the Spirit descended upon the people of Jerusalem at Pentecost, it unfolded as a gender-less experience. Although in Greek 'spirit' is a feminine noun, a good number of people use 'he' and 'she' almost interchangeably when referring to the Holy Spirit.

Mary at the heart of the new covenant

As well as Mary's role in popular religion, the second area in which I think Christians can speak confidently about Mary's continuing ministry takes us back to the idea of the *anawim* being a kind of remnant people who come into their own in the incarnation. It is to that moment of incarnation that we are able to trace back our own Christian spiritual roots. In Mary a new reality was initiated through a covenant between her and God. By implication, that new and renewing covenant must continue and in its continuation Mary still has a key role to play.

In the old covenant—that is, the deep and lasting relationships between God and his people in the period before Christ—we encounter a picture of a God who 'chooses' and of humans as being 'chosen' in order to be liberated. We see a series of encounters in which God and his people engage together in relationships of grace and of reciprocal love and faithfulness. However, something very important changes by the time the new covenant is initiated and God takes one mighty risk. The God who was once the 'chooser' now continues to choose but himself becomes one with the chosen by being incarnate. The risk was that the previously ordered relationship of covenant—a clear chooser and a clear chosen—becomes confused. By allowing the Word to become flesh, the inevitability of the cross and all that it entails overshadows the adventure of incarnation.

Under the old covenant Israel was the elect of God, chosen, however, not as a mere anonymous collection of people but given personal quality through its great representatives, in whom God looked upon the people as a whole, and whose duty it was to represent the people to God—Noah, Abraham,

Moses. Under the new covenant, the individual/nation tension is alleviated in two ways. First, the many representatives of the people of old were all forerunners of the one, final, and effective representative of men and women to God, for Jesus himself is the elect par excellence of God—he is the one promised; he is the Messiah; he is the anointed one.

Second, under the old covenant, we saw that Israel's response to God, when he first called that nation by his grace, was a response of total compliance with the will of God and a corresponding willingness to be led into freedom by him. At least this was the ideal, for Israel never really succeeded in living up to her calling. Under the new covenant, however, it is in the attitude of the Word made flesh, Jesus of Nazareth, that we can perceive the full realisation of this total and unconditional obedience to God's will.

By hearing Mary's 'yes' we encounter a further realisation of this obedience to God's will. In this way she represents the *anawim* of the past but also prefigures the *anawim* of the future, so that they too can become part of the adventure of a new covenant. In this respect, her continuing ministry encourages all Christians to encounter their own annunciation moments and be bold enough to say 'yes' to God.

We may notice a striking difference here—the people of the old covenant hung back, somewhat reluctant to get involved, while their leaders went forward obediently. In Mary, there is no such hanging back, and in her, heaven and earth finally converge and the finite encounters the infinite fully. Note that it is heaven that takes the initiative and bestows its infinity on the earth—the earth, thus endowed with infinity, responds accordingly and brings forth her fruit.

In the same spirit Mary, without knowing what would happen, accompanied her son through the events of his life, through the cross, through the darkness of death and on to resurrection. This sets a pattern for Mary's continuing journey of ministry, because through her we can see that the whole of God's action in Jesus Christ is the model for our own personal and spiritual involvement with God. In this way, we share in the work of liberating the world, thus moving all God's children closer towards a transfigured life.

In his seven volumes of theology *The Glory of the Lord* (T & T Clark, 1982–91) Hans Urs von Balthasar speaks in terms of Jesus being sown as a seed in the world, a seed that would flower as the Word of God. Although the Gospels have several images of seeds being sown and growing, for Balthasar the sowing of God's ultimate seed (Jesus) is less a historical process of growth and more an encounter of the world both with the Word made flesh and with subsequent radical changes that would happen as a result of this encounter. God sows the seed in the dark, dangerous, powerful womb of the world—but more immediately in the womb of Mary. Then the Word that Mary loves is sown again for all God's children through the birth in Bethlehem.

Incarnate, Jesus speaks of the seeds that are sown (Matthew 13:4–9, 18–23; 13:31–32; Mark 4:1–9, 13–20; Luke 8:4–8, 11–15) but it is only after his death and resurrection that these sayings are fully understood as referring to himself as the 'life-giving Word' (John 14:22–26; 16:25–28). After the resurrection, and as his followers recalled his actions on earth, his whole life came to be seen as an 'opening up' of seeds from which all could benefit. The Word of God must fall on ground that has been prepared; there must be a suitable vessel to receive the seed. Mary models that suitability for all time and so continues—albeit indirectly—to exercise a spiritual ministry of witness to God's people.

Journeys to where Mary is remembered

The third and final area in which I think Christians can speak of Mary as having a continuing ministry is by way of pilgrimage to physical places that continue to witness to her life. Books on places of pilgrimage associated with Mary (for example, Peter Mullen, *Shrines of Our Lady*, Piatkus, 1998) and on pilgrimage in general (for example, Andrew Jones, *Pilgrimage: The journey to remembering our story*, BRF, 2011) are in abundance. Over the years I have visited many such places where I have felt that Mary has at least an important inheritance and at best a vital continuing ministry. Four have made a particular impression on me. Earlier in this chapter I mentioned one of these—the shrine of Jasna Góra in Częstochowa, Poland. The other two are in England and in Spain and the third on my doorstep in Wales. To conclude this chapter, I want to revisit these places briefly, not so much on commenting specific details of the sites concerned as high-lighting one or two aspects of their spiritual heritage that may help us understand the idea of Mary's continuing presence a little better.

The English find Mary in Glastonbury

As we have seen, since the beginning of the Christian story people have been drawn to Mary for many different reasons and have subsequently visited places associated with her. Many of these Marian places of pilgrimage become missionary places—places primarily concerned with proclaiming the good news of the risen Christ, and many of us go to places such as Glastonbury to encounter the gospel values that Mary continues to pass on. What I found when I visited Glastonbury was a sense of profound 'changelessness' in the face of a fast-moving world of burgeoning technology, frightening uncertainties and a depth of complexity never before experienced. In my own pastoral ministry I have noticed how life's tenderness is so easily squeezed away in an era often characterised by an overwhelmingly brash and over-confident lifestyle. Since everyone has the personal experience of suffering, disquiet and grief at some point, the changelessness of Glastonbury—a place dedicated to the memory of Mary—helps modern pilgrims recognise and make sense of how they themselves have changed through their own experiences.

Glastonbury is possibly the oldest and most popular place of pilgrimage associated with Mary in England. In the contrast between Glastonbury's changelessness and people's spiritual and emotional ebbs and flows did I sense healing in that place.

A Spanish experience in Montserrat

Throughout the Bible, people climb mountains to seek God. Abraham, Moses, Elijah and David all experienced God's presence on a mountain. Jesus drew crowds up hills and revealed the power of God through his words and actions. Perhaps the most extraordinary mountain-top experience is the transfiguration, recorded in each of the Gospels and lying at the heart of Jesus' earthly ministry.

Like many people, I too have climbed mountains and encountered a glimpse of the eternal as Peter, James and John did that day on Mount Tabor when Jesus was transfigured before them. Perhaps my most striking mountain-top experience was at Montserrat in Spain, a mountain in the foothills of the Pyrenees, where, in a monastery, stands a wooden statue of Mary and Jesus called *La Moreneta* ('dark little one'). Tradition is that it was carved in Jerusalem when James was leader of the church there; his own shrine lies on the opposite shore of Spain in Santiago de Compostela. Millions of people visit this place annually and, as I did, describe it as a place of transfiguring power.

What does that really mean? Well, first, it refers to the strength received in particular places, which enables us to see the reflection of God in new and liberating ways, in other people and in the world. Secondly, it is, of course, an experience of worship, by which I mean that being at this place is itself a prayer. The more we get caught up in worshipping generously, the more we will experience the grace of God's transfiguring power; in other words, we will come to see things more as God sees them. We will realise that, as St Irenaeus (d. 202) said, the glory of God is men and women fully alive. Mary's continuing ministry at the top of Montserrat is that the memory of her enables pilgrims to do all of this—it certainly happened to me!

Mary on a Welsh peninsula

In the Christian tradition, peace is not merely the cessation or absence of hostilities. Its focus is on wholeness, harmony, well-being, prosperity and security. Throughout the Gospels it interconnects with the experience of love, particularly love for those who are different. It is worth noting that the first word of the crucified and risen Jesus to his disciples is 'peace' (Luke 24:36). It is no coincidence that modern-day pilgrims time and again travel in pursuit of that same wholeness, harmony, well-being, prosperity and security. This is why a pilgrimage is fundamentally different from a day out or a holiday on the beach. The latter can certainly provide rest and refreshment but a pilgrimage seeks to achieve more.

I live and work on an ancient pilgrimage route that meanders westwards along the Llŷn Peninsula in north-west Wales. Along the way pilgrims encounter a string of churches, wells, shrines and ancient stones as they journey to Bardsey Island (Ynys Enlli). Right at the tip of the peninsula and just before crossing a treacherous stretch of water, pilgrims encounter Mary. Even here, at a place that was once the most westerly edge of the Roman Empire, Mary has been commemorated for the best part of 1500 years. In a field above the valley down to the sea there once stood a church dedicated to Mary (the outline can still be seen) and you can climb down steps hewn out of the rock called *Grisiau Mair*, the 'steps of Mary'. At the bottom of the steps there is a well (St Mary's Well) where pilgrims have sought the protection of *Mair, Morwyn y Mor*, 'Mary, the virgin of the sea'. These ancient traditions connect to a time when Mary was, as is still the case in many places in the world, everyone's local saint. Her continuing gifts here are wholeness, harmony, well-being, prosperity and peace—a constant offering. That, for me, is physically expressed at the well, which overflows with clear fresh drinkable water even though it is covered by the sea twice daily!

Less about apparitions and more about the gospel

Finally, as a pilgrim to various places in the world, including shrines dedicated to Mary, I find myself—along with many others—less and less concerned with whether Mary (or, for that matter, any saint associated with specific sites) actually appeared there. Mary's continuing ministry is not about herself but about her son, Jesus Christ. As pilgrims journeying to the places of Mary, what matters is that we have the opportunity to respond to the power of the Holy Spirit, because pilgrimage is always an experience rooted and exercised in the Holy Spirit.

Those who go on pilgrimage should also have constant recourse to the Bible and read it in the awareness of what can be termed an 'eschatological tension' lying at the heart of the Gospel message. There is a balance between recognising that we are already walking the journey of life, very much in the kingdom, and, at the same time, acknowledging that part of that journey is not yet in the kingdom as the time of fulfilment is not quite here. Ultimately, true pilgrimage is always a journey from the heart of God and back to the heart of God. The journeys we make throughout our lives, on earth on our way back to that heart, offer amazing opportunities to experience the liberating and transfiguring power of God.

Chapter 8

Challenges from Christ's final prayer in John

'As you have sent me into the world, so I have sent them into the world. And for their sakes I sanctify myself, so that they also may be sanctified in truth. I ask not only on behalf of these, but also on behalf of those who will believe in me through their word, that they may all be one. As you, Father, are in me and I am in you, may they also be in us, so that the world may believe that you have sent me. The glory that you have given me I have given them, so that they may be one, as we are one, I in them and you in me, that they may become completely one, so that the world may know that you have sent me and have loved them even as you have loved me'.
JOHN 17:18–23

After the Last Supper, Jesus delivered what I often describe as the most powerful after-dinner speech ever (John 13:21—17:26)! He clearly recognises that the end of his earthly life is imminent and wants to underline the essential parts of his ministry. The speech ends with a rallying prayer for unity, a unity which is in two dimensions, vertical and horizontal. The vertical dimension grounds unity in the relationship between Jesus and God, and the horizontal sees in the command to love one another the expression of that relationship among members of the community.

Mary is sometimes discussed as if she was simply a divisive factor among Christians, but this is a huge oversimplification.

The person of Mary must lie at the heart of the theological issues surrounding ecumenism, for Christ did not simply drop down from heaven; he was born of a woman (Galatians 4:4). The faith of the Church is necessarily anchored in history, and Mary stands as a guarantee that the incarnation cannot be a marginal teaching. She is also the guarantee of the reality of human salvation: that God's grace reaches down into the roots of humanity and makes human beings holy before God, not in a future eternity but now.

Looking at the characters of the Bible, we realise that God chose some very unlikely people to bring about his purposes—and he still does. Nowhere is this seen more clearly than in the choice of Mary: a young, inexperienced and unknown girl from Galilee. Unlike God, most of us would never choose the likes of her to launch important ventures. But God did and how effective she was—a young woman with lots of humility and lots of grace: an unbeatable combination. It is true that various Christian traditions disagree about Mary's status, but let us try to hold on to the basics: God chose her to bring Christ into the world and at least to me that means she is pretty special! Whatever Christians of various denominations feel about Mary, I remain convinced that she cannot be left on the margins of any ecumenical dialogue, nor can we allow her to be a figure of contention. In this final chapter I want to focus on this issue and draw out the possibilities of recognising in Mary a figure not of contention but of profound unity.

Papal bulls and the Second Vatican Council

Admittedly, over the years not all discussions and decisions concerning Mary have been firmly rooted in the biblical witness in the strict sense of that phrase—and herein lies one of the main reasons for ecumenical discord regarding the figure of Mary. Two Roman Catholic dogmatic definitions in particular have caused concern in some parts of the Church. The first of these came in 1854 when Pope Pius IX issued the papal bull *Ineffabilis Deus* (God Ineffable), promulgating the doctrine of the Immaculate Conception. Basically, this declared that Mary, from the moment of her own conception, was completely sinless—even free from original sin—and remained so throughout her life. The second definition came in 1950 when Pope Pius XII issued a further papal bull *Munificentissus Deus* (Most Generous God), this time promulgating the doctrine of the Assumption. This declared that Mary, having completed her earthly life, was 'assumed', body and soul, into heaven after, as some Christian traditions believe, she fell asleep.

Both bulls have proved somewhat controversial over the years and have been at the centre of ecumenical conversations between the Roman Catholic Church and other Christian denominations throughout the world. The controversy concerning these two documents focused mainly on their Mariological, as opposed to Christological, emphasis and also on the fact that their basic claims were not substantiated by the biblical account. Having said that, in many ways one could argue that these two dogmatic definitions were the product of a 19th- and 20th-century Marian overenthusiasm, as well as a kind of ecclesial triumphalism on the part of the Roman Catholic Church; they were simply products of the age.

The 1854 and the 1950 definitions continued to have their supporters and even on the eve of the Second Vatican Council (1962–65) those supporters hoped for further dogmatic statements that were exclusively Marian, so as to offer 'new' definitions of Mary. But they were to be disappointed! In truth, the issuing of a new and exclusive document dealing with Mary had been contemplated and even presented in draft form to the Theological Commission of the Council in 1962. Jaroslav Pelikan describes how the Commission felt that to treat Mary in a separate document had dangers (*Mary Through the Ages*, Yale University Press, 1996). He notes how they were keen not to present Mary in isolation either from scripture or from the Church and to avoid both exaggeration and narrowness. In addition, the Commission was sensitive to wider ecumenical concerns as well as new biblical scholarship within Roman Catholic circles.

What eventually emerged from the Council was a very balanced summary of the various historical themes concerning Mary. Instead of being a separate treatment, it was included in the more general 1964 document *Lumen Gentium* (Light of All Nations) also known as 'The Dogmatic Constitution of the Church', dealing with a variety of church-related issues. The part of the document that dealt with Mary in relation to scripture and the Church fell into five sections:

- 'The Role of the Blessed Virgin Mary, Mother of God, in the Mystery of Christ and the Church': this focused on Mary as both divinely chosen and profoundly human.
- 'The Role of the Blessed Virgin Mary in the Economy of Salvation': this tended to concentrate on the biblical witness to Mary—both Old Testament and New Testament.
- 'The Blessed Virgin Mary and the Church': it is in this section that the Council explored the whole experience of the incarnation in relation to Mary.

- 'Devotion to the Blessed Virgin Mary in the Church': here the document focused on the various practices and exercises of devotion in relation to Mary.
- 'Mary, a Sign of Sure Hope and Solace for God's People in Pilgrimage': this final section explored Mary's ongoing ministry and recognised her as the mother of Jesus who continues in the present world as the image and first flowering of the Church.

In many ways the Second Vatican Council succeeded in offering Christian brothers and sisters of other traditions a crucial starting point for ecumenical dialogue and in a delicate way placed Mary at the very centre of Christian belief and practice. The bishops of the Council were only too aware that the various theological issues surrounding God, humanity, sin, salvation and grace all intertwine and are given a sharper focus by the theology of Mary. They realised that the ecumenical debate rests more securely on the nature of divine salvation than on Mariology alone—church teachings concerning Mary remain a facet of a much wider theological conversation. The outcome of the Second Vatican Council therefore placed Mary as being firmly of the Church and not above it.

A thaw between Rome and Canterbury

Ecumenical relationships between Rome and the Anglican Communion had already taken a turn for the better long before the commencement of the Second Vatican Council, through a series of crucial steps. The first of these was the resolution of the 1920 Lambeth Conference (the ten-yearly meeting of all Anglican bishops from the worldwide

Communion) appealing for Christian unity, albeit in a general way. Then came the visits of the Archbishops of Canterbury to the Popes in the Vatican—William Temple in 1944, Geoffrey Fisher in 1960, Michael Ramsey in 1966. Around these personal steps there was the founding of various bodies designed to move forward the quest for closer unity. In 1960 the Secretariat for Promoting Christian Unity (SPCU), which included non-Roman Catholic observers, was established in Rome under the leadership of Cardinal Bea, and in 1966 the Anglican Centre in Rome was founded.

Out of this emerged a highly significant body: the Anglican-Roman Catholic International Commission (ARCIC), which initially met to explore a variety of theological issues such as the Eucharist (1971) and ministry (1973). Both the 1971 and 1973 meetings led to an important climax in 1974 with a formal ecumenical statement known as ARCIC 1. This achieved above all both a sense of and a space for future ecumenical dialogue. Of course, there have been countless conversations and statements from many other meetings of Christian denominations but I stress the ARCIC meetings because in May 2005 a further ARCIC statement was issued that dealt solely with Mary.

Mary, grace and hope in Christ

The 2005 ARCIC 'Mary statement' ('Mary, grace and hope in Christ') can trace its roots back to 1981, when ARCIC 2 issued an agreed statement on 'Authority' within both churches. Section 30 of that report carried references to Mary and promised further joint reflection on the mother of our Lord. The 2005 report was a culmination of five years of study and reflection on Mary. Interestingly, the very beginning of the report notes that it is not an official statement of the Anglican Communion or the Roman Catholic Church, but that it does represent the sustained thinking of some major theologians as they studied together an important aspect of Christianity as believed down through the centuries. Above all else the document shows agreement concerning Christian faith and devotion related to Mary, who is portrayed and located firmly within the pattern of God's grace and hope. As such, it is therefore a powerful reflection of ecumenical efforts to seek out what can be held in common and to celebrate fundamental aspects of a common heritage.

The report showed that the Commission reached a consensus on five key points:

- That God has taken Mary in the fullness of her person into his glory and that this is consonant with scripture and can only be understood in the light of scripture. This shows that despite centuries of seemingly entrenched controversies, two Christian traditions find themselves closer here than they had hitherto thought.
- That by virtue of her being the mother of our Lord, Christ's own work of redemption reached back in Mary to the depths of her being and to her earliest beginnings. There is an eschatological ring to this—Christ welcoming into heaven his mother, through whom his work of salvation and redemption began.
- That what is stated by the Roman Catholic Church concerning the dogmas of Mary's Assumption into heaven and her Immaculate Conception is in fact consonant with scripture and ancient common traditions, when understood correctly within the biblical pattern of the economy of hope and grace.

- That when this agreed statement is fully accepted by the two communions, the dogmas of the Assumption and the Immaculate Conception can then be understood in a new ecumenical context.
- That Mary does have a continuing ministry which serves the ministry of the risen Christ, the unique mediator—part of which is to pray for the Church from her place in heaven, and that such a belief is not a divisive issue. There is a suggestion here that, although diversity continues to surround ideas about Mary, the breadth of that diversity is not such as to justify continued separation on other levels of our ecclesial life—potentially such as the Eucharist.

In his address given at the launch of the document at Westminster Abbey, the Anglican theologian and ARCIC participator Nicholas Sagovsky stated that, whether the 2005 Mary statement was fully accepted or not, the overwhelming gift of the project was its revealing of the remarkable convergence between Roman Catholic and Anglican theologians on issues that had been painfully divisive for too long. He recognised in the Mary statement a major step being taken towards a more stable unity between the churches. He added that during the years of study that led to the report, the insights of the Eastern Church had been particularly useful. In addition, aspects of Paul's letters had proved valuable as the project developed—reflecting on the place of Mary in the shared Christian faith in the light of Pauline themes of election, grace and hope (Romans 8:28) had been particularly inspiring. In this way, Mary is again seen as a 'type' of the whole Church as well as of the individual believer.

Now enter the Orthodox

Clearly, on the one hand, ARCIC is a formal conversation between Anglicans and Roman Catholics, but on the other hand it is part of a much bigger network of theological discourse taking place across denominational divides. In these ecumenical discussions, the Orthodox tradition is particularly significant, although there is an interesting and unexpected twist in the Orthodox approach to Mary. Undoubtedly, for Orthodox Christians Mary has always been regarded as the centre of church worship and piety as well as of personal and communal spirituality, but the irony is that there is very little systematic theological reflection on Mary. We could say that one of the main reasons for this is that Mary is too 'big' for such reflection and that in Orthodox thinking she is located at a very different level—the existential, experiential and vocational.

The Greek scholar, Nikos Nissiotis captures this well: 'When everything in church life speaks of and indicates Mary, including the structure of daily worship through a glorious worship and iconography, scholastic theology becomes superfluous or recognises that it is inadequate to deal with such a paramount event of immediate existential sharing of the faithful' (*Existentialism and Christian Faith*, University of Athens, 1956). For Nissiotis, any ecumenical approach to church life becomes crippled, overly anthropocentric and individualistic when Mary is left out. Without Mary, ecumenical hearts and minds that seek to unite in Christ through the one Spirit cannot truly come together.

The Orthodox Church therefore approved of the approach that the Second Vatican Council took concerning Mary, especially the way in which the Council placed Mary ecclesiologically and Christologically. The Council did not treat her in isolation from Christ and the Church and avoided dogmatic exaggerations while fully reaffirming her solidarity with the whole of the Christian community. However, the Orthodox approach to Mary is probably slightly more ambivalent to the 2005 ARCIC statement than to those made by the Second Vatican Council. The American Orthodox scholar John Jillions states that, while the careful tone of the ARCIC dialogue is, on the one hand, appreciated, it is, on the other hand, dissonant on the issue of the veneration of Mary ('Generations Call Her Blessed', *The Tablet*, 25 March 2006). For the Orthodox Church, such formal dogmas can potentially suffocate what is for them a far more emotional and spiritual theological approach. In a similar vein to what I said at the end of Chapter 5 about how Welsh theological reflection is focused through poetry and hymns, the Orthodox approach to Mary is best seen in its warm, generous and abundant iconography and spirituality. Over the centuries it has resisted making formal and systematic dogmatic pronouncements about Mary as mother of God, while wanting to preserve her place at the centre of the Church's heart.

And now the reformers

In some ways it is more difficult to talk in terms of a Protestant/Reformed view on specific theological and spiritual issues because the term 'Reformed' encompasses a huge spectrum of theological thinking and denominations. Even as the Reformed tradition was conceived, some of their influential thinkers and leaders held widely diverse views and as a result led groups of Christians in different directions.

During the 16th century Martin Luther, for instance, spearheaded the Reformation in one part of Europe with his particular agenda for doctrinal reform, while the more radical Swiss reformers Ulrich Zwingli and John Calvin took the movement in quite different and possibly more extreme directions. So while the Reformation changed the religious face of Europe, those changes differed according to particular personalities and geographical places. Interestingly, although itself a product of the Reformation, the Anglican Church (a widely dispersed communion of autonomous churches) had from its inception a number of instruments that ensured a major degree of uniformity—agreement on the validity of scripture, the Nicene Creed, the sacraments and the historic episcopate.

Although not reaching the same degree of uniformity as the Anglicans, during the 16th and 17th centuries the Reformed churches in various European countries produced their own national confessions, such as the Lutheran Augsburg Confession of 1530 and the Presbyterian Westminster Confession of 1643. These Confessions showed some important basic characteristics, four in particular:

- They insisted on a strong emphasis on the importance of Holy Scripture
- They stressed God's absolute sovereignty as opposed to any kind of human authority
- They were determined to underline, on the one hand, God's justification and sanctification of the believer, and on the other hand, that all this could only happen through personal faith
- They recognised Jesus, and him alone, as head of the church

Any theological exploration of Mary's role in the drama of God's salvific plan would not therefore seem possible—both because it was not necessary and because to do so would be seen as undoing some of the very principles that fuelled the Reformation in the first place. In recent years, however, there is a growing sense of new ecumenical opportunities and possibilities. Indeed, in 1995 there was an important Joint Statement produced by Methodists and Roman Catholics entitled 'Mary, Mother of the Lord, Sign of Grace, Faith and Holiness: Towards a shared understanding'. Although not an extensive document, it is the fruit of extensive theological reflection between these two churches. Right at the very beginning of the report the members of the joint group express their hope that the example of Mary as 'mother of our Lord' will inspire Christians to travel together, as pilgrims, in the journey of discerning and responding to God's will for their respective churches. They then take the pilgrimage metaphor further and express their conviction that Mary is indeed a model for all Christians in her own pilgrimage of faith.

What makes this Statement especially significant for me is the way in which two churches that clearly differ in their respective approaches to Mary do so honestly, openly and firmly from within a context of deep theological reflection. After all, any authentic ecumenical endeavour must begin from a place of truth and holiness. It is not in the ecumenical spirit to attempt to move forward from a place of embattled self-righteousness but rather from a place of respectful openness and mutual understanding.

Four aspects of this Statement make a particularly valuable contribution to discussion about the role of Mary as a less divisive and much more uniting figure.

- It recognises that Mary had a cooperative role with God in his work of redemption and as such remains a sign of what the Church is called to be and do. Like her, we contemporary disciples of Christ are called to play our part in cooperating with God's continuing work of redemption. We too have a role in witnessing to God's liberating and transfiguring power.
- By revealing where Methodists disagree with the Roman Catholic line, the Statement raises the crucial question of whether Methodists actually have as full an understanding of the biblical invitation for 'all generations' to call Mary 'blessed' as is theologically possible. Both scripture and Christian tradition are clear that Jesus was both human and divine, and that clarity is itself an enormously important statement about Mary. She was the mother who bore the Son of God and then went on to cherish him, shape him and continue witnessing to him.
- Inevitably, the Statement considers the theology of 'Justification', the doctrine that lies at the root of the original Reformation. There was agreement that those who are 'justified' and subsequently 'saved' are done so by grace *with* free consent and not saved *by* free consent. Salvation comes by way of God's grace but as God's children we are invited to cooperate with his grace—as Mary did by saying 'yes'. Just as God's children are called to become a sanctified people and to be made perfect in love, so the Statement agreed that Mary was entirely sanctified and by God's grace made perfect in love. It further states that 'Mary is a living proclamation of the mystery of God's grace and a perfect instance of the sovereign power of that grace'.
- The Statement does not shy away from the various ecumenical controversies surrounding the dogmas of the

Assumption and the Immaculate Conception. In a Catholic context both these dogmas emerged out of the tradition that Mary had the unique and high vocation to be the mother of the Son of God. While the Methodists accept that unique calling unreservedly, the dogmas, as they are represented in the Catholic Church, play no part in the Methodist ecclesiological scheme of things—they are simply not necessary.

Ultimately, I would argue that what is needed in the wider Churches' ecumenical approach to Mary is a balance between an Orthodox heart, a Roman Catholic reflection, an Anglican diversity and a Methodist generosity. With such a balance in place, perhaps we can then get closer to providing the world with a united and uniting icon of the face of Mary.

Our Lady of Kibeho

In Chapter 3 I wrote about the astonishing events that took place in Guadalupe in 1531, and the way in which that Mexican experience began a powerful ecumenical evangelising process (amazing, given the historical context) that resulted in new opportunities for dialogue and exploring different people's understanding of the image of God. In that context of evangelising ecumenism, new life and fresh unity touched the lives of many people. In 1531 Mary appeared to a poor Indian boy named Juan Diego, one of the *anawim* who stood for a people suffering extermination, enslavement and exploitation—a disgrace that was eventually reversed.

In 1981 Mary appeared to another group of *anawim*, on a different continent and almost 500 years apart, in a situation where the people were suffering a similar disgrace of extermination, enslavement and exploitation, again eventually reversed but not without the world first witnessing some of the worst genocidal atrocities ever. In 1994 the East African State of Rwanda experienced the mass slaughter of over 800,000 Tutsis by the Hutus in just over 100 days. It was the culmination of longstanding ethnic competition and tension between the minority Tutsi peoples, who had held power for centuries, and the majority Hutu peoples, who had come to power in the rebellion of 1959–62.

In 1990 the Rwandan Patriotic Front (RPF)—a rebel group composed mostly of Tutsi refugees—invaded northern Rwanda from Uganda in a direct attempt to defeat the Hutu-led government, thus beginning a cruel and horrific civil war. It was the assassination of Juvenal Habyarimana, the Hutu leader, in April 1994, that set off a violent reaction during which Hutu groups conducted the mass genocide of hundreds of thousands of Tutsis. At the time the media zoomed into homes all over the world horrific images of Hutus killing Tutsis, babies and children openly slaughtered, women publicly raped before being decapitated, streets littered with bodies and piles of skulls and bones. One edition of *Time* magazine reported that year: 'There were no devils left in hell, they were all in Rwanda' and young Rwandan boys were heard chanting in the streets an old Rwandan proverb: 'Death is hungry and is never full.'

One of the worst atrocities associated with the genocide happened in Kibeho in south-west Rwanda, where thousands of people had gathered in and around the local Catholic parish church and where, according to some estimates, over 5000 people were massacred in a single attack. They had gathered there primarily because it was already a well-known and popular place of Christian pilgrimage and reconciliation—not only for African Christians but also for Europeans and Americans. Over a number of years following 1981 several Marian apparitions had taken place there and Mary had appeared to a small number of young school children with the name 'Nyina wa Jambo' (Mother of the Word). The apparitions communicated various messages, including an almost apocalyptic vision of Rwanda descending into violence and hatred—possibly foretelling the 1994 Rwandan genocide. In the vision of 19 August 1982 the children involved unanimously reported seeing violence, dismembered bodies and mass destruction.

In the apparitions the children all reported hearing Mary calling them back to God and asking them to share her message: 'Pray for one another, love each other and show no hypocrisy; forgive and be changed.' One of the people who continued to spread the message of Kibeho is Immaculée Ilibagiza, from the village of Mataba close to Kibeho. She survived the 1994 genocide by spending 91 days hiding in a cramped bathroom that belonged to the local priest. Apart from one brother, she lost her complete family.

In 2007 she was the recipient of the International Mahatma Gandhi Reconciliation and Peace Award and in two of her books (*Left to Tell*, Hay House, 2006, and *Our Lady of Kibeho*, Hay House, 2008) she shares how her faith guided her through the terrible ordeal and she describes her eventual forgiveness of and compassion towards her family's killers.

By today Kibeho has gained the reputation of being a place of new spiritual significance: it is a place not only of suffering but also of purification and joy. Since the dark days of the mid-1990s more and more pilgrims have gathered there to remember that, while they are unable to change the past, they can turn to God now and give thanks for the message of Mary. One of the lasting gifts of Kibeho is that it is now a place where the Hutu peoples and Tutsi peoples gather together to worship and to repent. In the same spirit as Guadalupe, Kibeho continues to provide exciting opportunities for peoples of different traditions to grapple with understanding the meaning of God and his ways in the world. It is a place that opens up spaces for those from very different contexts to gather together regularly as one.

God once spoke his Word through Mary, and, for many Christians, Mary continues to speak God's word to the *anawim* of today's world—whether that be in Guadalupe, Lourdes, Fatima, Walsingham or Kibeho in Rwanda. As this book comes to a close, I am certain of one thing—as Christ prayed for unity in his after-dinner speech on that Thursday evening in an upstairs room in a house in Jerusalem, it would have been a prayer for the kind of liberating power and transfiguring reconciliation that we encounter in places like Kibeho.

Afterword

Writing this book has been an amazing journey for me. I started this journey towards Mary not knowing exactly where it would lead me and slightly nervous that there would not be enough material for a whole book! I have always enjoyed a warm relationship with the idea of Mary but this last year has changed that and it has become less of a warm idea and more of a lasting commitment. If you were to ask me, 'Commitment to what?', I am not sure I could answer the question, but I think it has something to do with the Orthodox heart I mentioned in Chapter 8; less about spelling it out and much more about feeling it.

My journey has not ended yet because I want to take it further—much further. I have written elsewhere about the difference between a pilgrim and a tourist: tourists pass through a particular place but pilgrims allow the place to pass through them. In writing this book, I actually feel I have been on a pilgrimage, because I have not merely 'passed through' places and events connected with Mary. During this past year those 'Mary places' and 'Mary events' have changed me and I am excited about where the pilgrimage might take me next.

I started the book by looking at the songs of Hebrew children and I want to end with the idea of song. As a child Jesus may well have heard his mother singing to him. As we know, she did sing a revolutionary kind of song which is recorded for us in Luke's Gospel (Luke 1:46–55). In it she sang about neighbourliness—about how God brings down the mighty from their thrones and lifts up the lowly.

She sang about how God fills the hungry with good things and sends the rich away empty. Mary did not make up this dangerous song; she took it from another mother, Hannah (1 Samuel 2:1–10). It was an old song and probably quite well known. Hannah may well have sung it to her son Samuel, who became one of ancient Israel's greatest revolutionaries by overseeing a significant change of leadership from one that was loosely held together through the Israelites' common origin to the establishment of monarchy. Hannah, Mary and their respective young boys all imagined a radical social transformation—and Jesus enacted his mother's song at every given opportunity. Everywhere he went he broke the vicious cycle of poverty, bondage, fear and death. He healed, transformed, empowered and brought new life. Jesus' example gives us the mandate to transform our own public life, working to make transfiguration and liberation an ongoing reality.

Performing 'wonders and signs' was another way in which Jesus enacted his mother's song. Everywhere Jesus visited during his public ministry the world was transfigured and set free—the blind received their sight, the lame walked, the lepers were cleansed, the deaf heard, the dead were raised and the poor freed from debt. Jesus constantly left ordinary people dazzled, amazed and grateful but he left powerful people angry and upset, because every time he performed a wonder, the spiritual and social bullies lost a little of their clout. The wonders of the new age of the coming of God's kingdom will certainly dazzle us but also, I suspect, make us nervous, even scandalise and upset some of us. The people of God need help in processing this ambivalent sense of both yearning for God's new creation and deeply fearing it. It is one thing to pray 'your kingdom come' (Luke 11:2) but a completely different thing to be ready to greet the kingdom now.

Such processing will mean clearing away ecclesiastical clutter that has accumulated over the years and got in the way of interpreting scripture creatively and living the Gospel authentically. It will sometimes mean asking tough and threatening questions and firing theological torpedoes. Such action is needed, not to destroy the roots from which divine revelation is nourished or the essential truths of the liberating and transfiguring gospel, but to destroy some of the rigid structures of the Church that obscure that revelation and send the wrong people away empty.

One of the writers whom I have found particularly inspiring in this journey of Mary is the Dutch feminist theologian I have already mentioned, Catharina Halkes. In one of her books she reflects on Mary's song as being in the prophetic tradition (*Mary and Women*, Concilium, 1983). The suggestion that Mary stands in a long line of prophets is particularly fruitful and salutary when we balance Mary's 'yes' against the song that she sings. In other words, our own cooperation in the liberating work of God cannot remain a static ideology—and that applies to us as individual Christians and to the Church as a whole. As missional co-workers with God, we have to remain open and accessible to the transfiguring power of the Holy Spirit. Then our ministry becomes both authentic and prophetic.

When we ourselves are inspired by Mary's song, we become more conscious of the exemplary attitude of faith expressed in Mary's 'yes', and we can make it a reality by emptying ourselves of our prejudices and hypocrisy. Saying 'yes' is not about serving 'the needy' condescendingly and stooping down benevolently to help the poor. Rather, it is about being in complete and honest solidarity with the poor, the silent, the marginalised, the spiritually, emotionally and physically hungry and the suffering people of our world—today's *anawim*, wherever they are to be found.

Questions for group discussion and reflection

Chapter 1: Songs and cries of Hebrew children

- Too often nowadays the word 'poor' is synonymous with those who are financially challenged. *Anawim* is a word that I use often in this book to describe those who were poor—in every sense of that word—and who attracted the favour of the prophets and for whom God had a 'soft spot'. Who then would you consider to be the *anawim* of today? Why and in what ways do they, in their poverty, help us to understand God a little better?
- The original ark of the covenant contained the precious commandments of God, carried around Israel by the Judges as a symbol of unity among the tribes of Israel. Compare what is said about that ark in 2 Samuel 6 with the idea of Mary as the new ark of the covenant, carrying an even more precious gift (Luke 1:26–38)—a gift that offered the possibility of an eternal unity. Reflect on that connection and the ways in which you understand the gift of Jesus' birth as a source of unity.
- Imagine yourself as a pilgrim in Jerusalem who happened to be in the temple precinct when Mary arrived there with Joseph and her baby boy (Luke 2:22–32). Create a picture—either in words or by drawing—of the scene. When you hear the words of Simeon to Mary, in what ways do you feel that this was fulfilment? What was being fulfilled and by whom?

Chapter 2: New Testament variations on Mary

- What is (or was) your initial reaction to the fact that so little is actually said in the Gospels about Mary? Imagine yourself as a well-heeled pilgrim, having travelled to many pilgrimage places that are associated with Mary—Walsingham, Lourdes, Fatima, for instance—but never having thought much about the New Testament brevity regarding Mary. Does this fact affect your perception of these places? If so, in what ways? If not, why?
- Spend some time reading the references to Mary in the Gospels of Matthew, Mark and Luke. What do you make of the variations and why do you think the evangelists had such different agendas concerning Mary?
- Why do you think John's Gospel never mentions Mary by name? Do you see a link here with the Last Supper, where, unlike the other Gospels, John does not use the words, 'Do this in remembrance of me'? Is John assuming that his original readers had sufficient knowledge so as to be able to 'read between the lines'?

Chapter 3: Divinely chosen, kingdom worker

- Many people, particularly in places of injustice and suffering, seek freedom and liberation, and liberation theology has proved very helpful in such contexts. How can Mary—her role, her qualities, her reputation—help those who are in need? To what extent can the Gospel picture of Mary help women in their struggles for respect and equality? Is your perception of that picture too gentle to make a difference?
- How do you react to claims made by Christians in many parts of the world that Mary has physically appeared in

places such as Guadalupe in Mexico? If you have visited such a place, what effect did it have on you? How has this chapter helped to inform your understanding and appreciation of such apparitions?

- How central is the biblical portrayal of incarnation—that God the creator and redeemer of all entered our world through Mary and in the person of Jesus—to your spiritual life? How do you think incarnation impacts on the daily life of the world?

Chapter 4: Virgin mother, profoundly human

- Compare the accounts of the birth of Jesus in the Gospels of Matthew (1:18–25) and Luke (2:1–20) and discuss the way they differ. How important is it that Mary was a virgin?
- I talk about paradox and how the incarnation itself can be seen as a paradox—one moment a king, next moment dying the death of a thief on the cross; one moment glory, next moment humiliation; one moment God, next moment man. What do you make of these paradoxes and how far do you recognise that strength can indeed be discovered in weakness and vulnerability? To what extent does the Church today recognise its primary vocation as a body called to serve and not to rule?
- There is a popular perception that Roman Catholics 'worship' Mary, but she is actually venerated because she points us to Christ. How do you feel that your perceptions of Mary are changing as you read this book?

Chapter 5: Light shining from Nazareth

- Over the years a great deal of attention has been paid to Mary's 'yes'. How influential is her 'yes' for our own saying 'yes' to God's call? In what different circumstances do we have the opportunity to say yes to God? Are there times when we say 'no' to God, and if so, what may the reasons and consequences be?
- In John's Gospel Mary is strategically placed at the beginning and at the end of Jesus' life. What statement do you think John is trying to make here? In what ways do you find this strategic continuity useful and effective?
- We all do our theological thinking and reflection in different ways. I mentioned the Welsh *plygain* carols and the way in which they focus on both the manger and the cross. Have a look at some of the popular English carols and identify various aspects of them (some verses maybe) that succeed in capturing the real power and meaning behind the light that shines from Nazareth (and Bethlehem).

Chapter 6: Anguish at the foot of the cross

- How do you react to the way in which John portrays the crucifixion as the moment of glory and exaltation as opposed to the moment of humiliation? Compare the scene of the cross in John's Gospel with the scene portrayed in the other Gospels. Which portrayal best speaks to you and why?
- I mentioned the 'birthday of the Church' on a number of occasions—the possibility of it being at the manger, or in the upper room, or at the empty tomb or at Pentecost. Do you agree with me that the birthday of the Church is seen at the foot of the cross, where we have community,

compassion and commitment? If so, then why? If not, then where do you see the birthday?

- As Mary gazed upon the cross, do you think she saw ruin or hope? Was there a crack through which a light could be seen that Friday afternoon on Calvary? How important do you think it is to read the whole story together—whatever the story? The whole of Jesus' story brings together Nazareth, Bethlehem, Calvary, the empty tomb and the Jerusalem of Pentecost. How do you interpret the connections between these places and the events that happened?

Chapter 7: Witnessing God's transfiguring power

- Take another look at Mary's song in Luke 1 and divide it into two: vv. 46–50 and vv. 51–55. Do you agree that we tend to overstate the second part and neglect the first? If so, why do we do this? Clearly, the second part relates well to the liberationist approach to the gospel but the first part tells us that Mary will be remembered for ever. What does that mean for you?
- I mention Mary's continuing ministry. How do you react to that phrase? If you react positively, what do you think is her continuing ministry today? If you react negatively, why do you feel that there is no need for a continuing ministry, and how do you understand v. 48?
- Have you ever been on a pilgrimage? If so, reflect on the journey in relation to what this chapter has to say about places and the importance of place. Whether you have been on a pilgrimage or not, it is certainly a useful metaphor for all our life journeys—even daily journeys. Each journey we make involves preparation, travel,

arriving and returning. Luke's Gospel suggests that the pilgrimage of life starts with God and ends in God—that's where Luke (like all other the Gospel writers) begins and ends his story. In what ways do you understand our journey of life as beginning in God and ending in him? What is the real purpose of the middle bit that we call life on earth?

Chapter 8: Challenges from Christ's final prayer in John

- Look again at part of what I call 'the best after-dinner speech ever delivered': John 13:21—17:26. Jesus knew the end was at hand and so he sat his disciples down one more time and highlighted the most important bits of what they had experienced together. What do you see as the highlights of that speech? What is it that Jesus truly wants his disciples to remember? The final part of the speech is Jesus' prayer for unity. How important is the ecumenical movement for you? How do you contribute to Christian unity?
- In working towards Christian unity, is the person of Mary for you a uniting force or something that remains divisive? Articulate your view by offering constructive reasons.
- I offered a summary of some aspects of the approach of different churches to Mary. Would you agree that we need an authentic balance between an Orthodox heart, a Catholic reflection, an Anglican diversity and a Methodist generosity? What are your opinions on the various ecumenical conversations concerning Mary, and with which church emphasis would you align yourself?

References

The New Testament references to Mary

Galatians 4:4: Paul refers to Christ as being 'born of a woman'
Mark 3:31–35: Jesus contrasts his disciples with his family
Mark 6:3: The people of Nazareth identify Jesus' family
Matthew 1:1—2:23: The genealogy, conception and birth of Jesus
Luke 1:26–56: The annunciation, Mary's visit to Elisabeth, Mary's song of praise
Luke 2:1–52: The birth and presentation of Jesus, Jesus in Jerusalem aged twelve
John 2:1–12: The wedding at Cana
John 7:41–42; 8:41: The origins of Jesus
John 19:25–27: Mary at the foot of the cross
Acts 1:14: The disciples gather to pray after the Ascension
Revelation 12:16: A vision of the woman giving birth to the Messiah

The feasts and commemorations of Mary

1 January: The Solemnity of Mary, Mother of God

This celebration is meant to commemorate the part played by Mary in the mystery of salvation by exalting God's redeeming work. It is also an opportunity for renewing our adoration of the newborn prince of peace and listening once more to the glad tidings of the angels and receiving the message of peace.

2 February: The Purification of Mary and Presentation of the Lord

This is a joint commemoration of the Son and of the mother and celebrates a mystery of salvation with which Mary was intimately associated as mother of the suffering Son of God and as one who performs a mission that belongs to the expectations of ancient Israel.

11 February: Our Lady of Lourdes

This feast celebrates the appearance of Mary to St Bernadette in 1858. It focuses specifically on Mary's prayers for the sick and the suffering and regards her as the comforter of the afflicted.

19 March: The husband of Mary—Joseph

Christians have celebrated this feast since 1324 but subsequent popes (Pius IX in 1870 and Leo XIII in 1889) attached to this feast the importance of recognising Joseph as patron of the universal Church, as a model for fathers and as the ideal worker.

25 March: The Annunciation of the Lord

Celebrated nine months before Christmas, this is another joint feast of Christ and his mother. It focuses on Mary's 'yes' and as such commemorates the beginning of the indissoluble union of the divine nature of Christ with human nature.

13 May: Our Lady of Fatima

This feast commemorates the appearance of Mary to three children on five subsequent occasions in 1917. She asked the children to pray the rosary prayer and to build a chapel. The feast focuses on the traditional 'threefold message of Fatima', namely, the practice of penance, the praying of the rosary and devotion to Mary.

31 May: The Visitation of Mary to Elizabeth

This feast recalls Mary, carrying her son in her womb, visiting Elizabeth to offer help and to proclaim the mercy of God the Saviour.

After Pentecost: The Immaculate Heart of Mary

Following the appearances of Mary at Fatima, Pope Pius XII consecrated the world to the Immaculate Heart of Mary in 1942 and two years later established the feast for the universal Church. The theme of the celebration is the call to become worthy temples of God's glory. It falls on the Saturday following the second Sunday after Pentecost. Associated with this feast is the practice of beginning each day with a prayer, the 'morning offering', by which we offer the day to God and accepts, as from the hands of God, all that comes to us in its course.

16 July: Our Lady of Mount Carmel

This feast was instituted about 1380 by the Carmelites in thanksgiving for the order's successful establishment in the West, having been forced to leave their place of origin (Mount Carmel in the Holy Land). The celebration encourages Christians to hold up Mary as a model of prayer, contemplation and dedication to God.

15 August: The Assumption of Mary

This feast encourages Christians to renew their joy in the destiny of Mary and all who belong to the risen Christ. In the papal bull which promulgated this feast no position is taken as to whether Mary actually died or not, but the faith of the Roman Catholic Church declared that Mary, in the fullness of her historical personality, now lives in union with the risen Christ, her son.

22 August: Our Lady, Queen and Mother

Catholic tradition claims that after her assumption, Mary was crowned Queen of Heaven. This feast contemplates Mary, who, seated beside God, shines as queen and intercedes as mother.

8 September: The Birthday of the Blessed Virgin Mary

Like any other birthday, this feast is a celebration of the gift of life—in this case, Mary's life.

15 September: Our Lady of Sorrows

This feast recalls the sorrows of Mary at the foot of the cross and is seen as a fitting occasion for reliving a decisive moment in the history of salvation and for venerating, together with her Son lifted up on the cross, his suffering mother. The theme of the celebration is union with Christ in his sufferings. Catholic tradition mentions the 'Seven Sorrows of Mary': Simeon's prophecy, the flight into Egypt, the loss of the holy child in the temple, meeting Jesus on the way to Calvary, the crucifixion, the descent from the cross and the burial.

24 September: Our Lady of Ransom

This feast was originally linked to the Order of Mercedarians, which was established in 1218 to work for the liberation of slaves, and focused on Mary's prayers and compassion for all slaves.

7 October: Our Lady of the Rosary

This feast was instituted in 1573 as a special commemoration of the victory gained at Lepanto in 1571 over the forces of Islam threatening to invade Europe. The theme of the celebration is the call to follow Christ by living his joyful, sorrowful and glorious mysteries in union with Mary.

21 November: The Presentation of the Blessed Virgin Mary

This ancient feast was based on a pious tradition, recounted in the *Protoevangelium* of James, that Mary was presented in the temple of Jerusalem at the age of three where she lived with other girls in the charge of holy women. The theme of this feast is the call to consecrate our lives to God as Mary did.

28 November: Our Lady of Kibeho

This is a feast that is not universally celebrated but is local to Rwanda. It commemorates the appearance of Mary in Kibeho and is a call for people to be reconciled.

8 December: The Immaculate Conception

This feast stems from the 1854 papal bull that centres upon the victory of God's grace freely given in Christ. It declared that the whole human race is offered salvation through God's mercy in the life, death and resurrection of Christ before any good works on our part. God's victory over sin is celebrated as Mary is conceived and her pure union with Christ established.

12 December: Our Lady of Guadalupe

This feast commemorates the way Mary appeared to Juan Diego on Mount Tepeyac in Mexico in 1531. She was declared

'Patroness of all Latin America' by Pope Pius X and 'Queen of Mexico and Empress of the Americas' by Pope Pius XII. The theme of the celebration centres on the way in which Mary unites and reconciles American Catholic—North and South.

25 December: The Nativity of Our Lord

Mary is regarded as a central figure in the birth narratives and as such is a key player in our Christmas celebrations.

30 December: The Holy Family

On this feast the Church meditates profoundly upon the holy life led by Jesus and his parents in the house at Nazareth. Its focus is mainly on the importance of the gift of family life—its communion of love, its simple beauty and its sacred and inviolable character.

Also by Andrew Jones

Pilgrimage

The journey to remembering our story

The age-old practice of pilgrimage is more popular than it has been for centuries. At a time when the Church seems increasingly exiled and estranged from our culture, more and more people are treading the ancient pilgrim routes, whether they are committed Christians, spiritual seekers or simply curious. The renewal of faith that they find on their journey often outweighs what happens in many churches.

Andrew Jones shows how pilgrimage can awaken those at all stages of belief to remembering the story of God's creating and redeeming work in history, which tells us who we are, where we have come from and where we are going. The act of remembering it not only offers a life-transforming way out of exile but points to the way home, to the place where we can live authentic and balanced lives. The book concludes with a focus on eight popular places of pilgrimage in the British Isles, drawing lessons from their history and spiritual heritage that can encourage and inspire us on our own faith journeys.

Also from BRF

The Sacred Place of Prayer

The human person created in God's image

Jean Marie Dwyer

There are many books available on the subject of prayer, so why add another one? The uniqueness of Jean Marie Dwyer's approach is the conviction that prayer, even contemplative prayer, is natural to everyone because we are created for God and reflect God… As created humans, we are the sacred place of prayer.

What does that mean? In the first three chapters she explores in a very accessible style the philosophical, biblical and theological groundwork for the understanding of the human person as the sacred place of prayer before moving on to consider what it means to be a contemplative.

Within us all is a deep need for love and a place of belonging. Jean Marie's chapters on desert spirituality, illusions and finding our centre give insight into how we find our true self and our place of home and belonging through prayer. The book concludes by considering Mary, the mother of Jesus.

ISBN 978 0 85746 241 1 £6.99
Available from your local Christian bookshop or direct from BRF: visit www.brfonline.org.uk

Also available on Kindle

Also from BRF

Hilda of Whitby

A spirituality for now

Ray Simpson

If you believe history to be dry and irrelevant, Aidan and Hilda Community founder Ray Simpson encourages you to think again by considering the life of an almost forgotten heroine of the early centuries of Christianity in England, Hilda of Whitby.

Ray unfolds the story of Hilda's work at Hartlepool and Whitby, drawing key lessons for our own age from her life, work and legacy and through questions for reflection, encourages personal application. Just before her birth, Hilda's mother had a vision of light cast from a necklace across Britain—a vision that St Bede, writing in the *Ecclesiastical History of the English People*, regarded as being fulfilled through Hilda. This light Ray Simpson projects now, 1400 years later, into our own age.

Enjoyed this book?

Write a review—we'd love to hear what you think.
Email: reviews@brf.org.uk

Keep up to date—receive details of our new books as they happen.
Sign up for email news and select your interest groups at:
www.brfonline.org.uk/findoutmore/

Follow us on Twitter @brfonline

By post—to receive new title information by post (UK only), complete the form below and post to: BRF Mailing Lists, 15 The Chambers, Vineyard, Abingdon, Oxfordshire, OX14 3FE

Your Details

Name ______________________________
Address ______________________________
____
Town/City ____________________ Post Code __________
Email ______________________________

Your Interest Groups (*Please tick as appropriate)

- ❑ Advent/Lent
- ❑ Bible Reading & Study
- ❑ Children's Books
- ❑ Discipleship
- ❑ Leadership
- ❑ Messy Church
- ❑ Pastoral
- ❑ Prayer & Spirituality
- ❑ Resources for Children's Church
- ❑ Resources for Schools

Support your local bookshop
Ask about their new title information schemes.